Eat to Live

Quick, and Delicious Recipes

Sharon J. Cuthbertson

FRENCH TERMS used in modern Household Cookery, explained.

ASPIC.—A savoury jelly, used as an exterior moulding for cold game, poultry, fish, &c. This, being of a transparent nature, allows the article which it covers to be seen through it. This may also be used for decorating or garnishing.

ASSIETTE (plate).—*Assiettes* are the small *entrées* and *hors-d'œuvres*, the quantity of which does not exceed what a plate will hold. At dessert, fruits, cheese, chestnuts, biscuits, &c., if served upon a plate, are termed *assiettes*.—ASSIETTE VOLANTE is a dish which a servant hands round to the guests, but is not placed upon the table. Small cheese soufflés and different dishes, which ought to be served very hot, are frequently made *assiettes volantes*.

AU-BLEU.—Fish dressed in such a manner as to have a *bluish* appearance.

BAIN-MARIE.—An open saucepan or kettle of nearly boiling water, in which a smaller vessel can be set for cooking and warming. This is very useful for keeping articles hot, without altering their quantity or quality. If you keep sauce, broth, or soup by the fireside, the soup reduces and becomes too strong, and the sauce thickens as well as reduces; but this is prevented by using the *bain-marie*, in which the water should be very hot, but not boiling.

BÉCHAMEL.—French white sauce, now frequently used in English cookery.

BLANCH.—To whiten poultry, vegetables, fruit, &c., by plunging them into boiling water for a short time, and afterwards plunging them into cold water, there to remain until they are cold.

BLANQUETTE.—A sort of fricassee.

BOUILLI.—Beef or other meat boiled; but, generally speaking, boiled beef is understood by the term.

BOUILLIE.—A French dish resembling hasty-pudding.

BOUILLON.—A thin broth or soup.

BRAISE.—To stew meat with fat bacon until it is tender, it having previously been blanched.

BRAISIÈRE.—A saucepan having a lid with ledges, to put fire on the top.

BRIDER.—To pass a packthread through poultry, game, &c., to keep together their members.

CARAMEL (burnt sugar).—This is made with a piece of sugar, of the size of a nut, browned in the bottom of a saucepan; upon which a cupful of stock is gradually poured, stirring all the time, and adding the broth little by little. It may be used with the feather of a quill, to colour meats, such as the upper part of fricandeaux; and to impart colour to sauces. Caramel made with water instead of stock may be used to colour *compôtes* and other *entremets*.

CASSEROLE.—A crust of rice, which, after having been moulded into the form of a pie, is baked, and then filled with a fricassee of white meat or a purée of game.

COMPÔTE.—A stew, as of fruit or pigeons.

CONSOMMÉ.—Rich stock, or gravy.

CROQUETTE.—Ball of fried rice or potatoes.

CROÛTONS.—Sippets of bread.

DAUBIÈRE.—An oval stewpan, in which *daubes* are cooked; *daubes* being meat or fowl stewed in sauce.

DÉSOSSER.—To *bone,* or take out the bones from poultry, game, or fish. This is an operation requiring considerable experience.

Entrées.—Small side or corner dishes served with the first course.

Entremets.—Small side or corner dishes served with the second course.

Escalopes.—Collops; small, round, thin pieces of tender meat, or of fish, beaten with the handle of a strong knife to make them tender.

Feuilletage.—Puff-paste.

Flamber.—To singe fowl or game, after they have been picked.

Foncer.—To put in the bottom of a saucepan slices of ham, veal, or thin broad slices of bacon.

Galette.—A broad thin cake.

Gâteau.—A cake, correctly speaking; but used sometimes to denote a pudding and a kind of tart.

Glacer.—To glaze, or spread upon hot meats, or larded fowl, a thick and rich sauce or gravy, called *glaze*. This is laid on with a feather or brush, and in confectionary the term means to ice fruits and pastry with sugar, which glistens on hardening.

Hors-d'œvres.—Small dishes, or *assiettes volantes* of sardines, anchovies, and other relishes of this kind, served to the guests during the first course. (*See* Assiettes volantes.)

Lit.—A bed or layer; articles in thin slices are placed in layers, other articles, or seasoning, being laid between them.

Maigre.—Broth, soup, or gravy, made without meat.

Matelote.—A rich fish-stew, which is generally composed of carp, eels, trout, or barbel. It is made with wine.

Mayonnaise.—Cold sauce, or salad dressing.

Menu.—The bill of fare.

Meringue.—A kind of icing, made of whites of eggs and sugar, well beaten.

Miroton.—Larger slices of meat than collops; such as slices of beef for a vinaigrette, or ragoût or stew of onions.

Mouiller.—To add water, broth, or other liquid, during the cooking.

Paner.—To cover with very fine crumbs of bread, meats, or any other articles to be cooked on the gridiron, in the oven, or frying-pan.

Piquer.—To lard with strips of fat bacon, poultry, game, meat, &c. This should always be done according to the vein of the meat, so that in carving you slice the bacon across as well as the meat.

Poelée.—Stock used instead of water for boiling turkeys, sweetbreads, fowls, and vegetables, to render them less insipid.—This is rather an expensive preparation.

Purée.—Vegetables or meat reduced to a very smooth pulp, which is afterwards mixed with enough liquid to make it of the consistency of very thick soup.

Ragoût.—Stew or hash.

Remoulade.—Salad dressing.

Rissoles.—Pastry, made of light puff-paste, and cut into various forms, and fried. They may be filled with fish, meat, or sweets.

Roux.—Brown and white; French thickening.

Salmi.—Ragoût of game previously roasted.

Sauce Piquante.—A sharp sauce, in which somewhat of a vinegar flavour predominates.

Sauter.—To dress with sauce in a saucepan, repeatedly moving it about.

Tamis.—Tammy, a sort of open cloth or sieve through which to strain broth and sauces, so as to rid them of small bones, froth, &c.

Tourte.—Tart. Fruit pie.

TROUSSER.—To truss a bird; to put together the body and tie the wings and thighs, in order to round it for roasting or boiling, each being tied then with packthread, to keep it in the required form.

VOL-AU-VENT.—A rich crust of very fine puff-paste, which may be filled with various delicate ragoûts or fricassees, of fish, flesh, or fowl. Fruit may also be inclosed in a *vol-au-vent*.

FRITTERS, Indian.

Ingredients.—3 tablespoonfuls of flour, boiling water, the yolks of 4 eggs, the whites of 2, hot lard or clarified dripping, jam. *Mode.*—Put the flour into a basin, and pour over it sufficient *boiling* water to make it into a stiff paste, taking care to stir and beat it well, to prevent it getting lumpy. Leave it a little time to cool, and then break into it (*without beating them at first*) the yolks of 4 eggs and the whites of 2, and stir and beat all well together. Have ready some boiling lard or butter; drop a dessertspoonful of batter in at a time, and fry the fritters of a light brown. They should rise so much as to be almost like balls. Serve on a dish, with a spoonful of preserve or marmalade dropped in between each fritter. This is an excellent dish for a hasty addition to dinner, if a guest unexpectedly arrives, it being so easily and quickly made, and it is always a great favourite. *Time.*—From 5 to 8 minutes to fry the fritters. *Average cost*, exclusive of the jam, 5*d*. *Sufficient* for 4 or 5 persons. *Seasonable* at any time.

FRITTERS, Plain.

Ingredients.—3 oz. of flour, 3 eggs, 1/3 pint of milk. *Mode.*—Mix the flour to a smooth batter with a small quantity of the milk; stir in the eggs, which should be well whisked, and then the remainder of the milk; beat the whole to a perfectly smooth batter, and should it be found not quite thin enough, add two or three tablespoonfuls more milk. Have ready a frying-pan, with plenty of boiling lard in it; drop in rather more than a tablespoonful at a time of the batter and fry the fritters a nice brown, turning them when sufficiently cooked on one side. Drain them well from the greasy moisture by placing them upon a piece of blotting-paper before the fire; dish them on a white d'oyley, sprinkle over them sifted sugar, and send to table with them a cut lemon and plenty of pounded sugar. *Time.*—From 6 to 8 minutes. *Average cost*, 4*d*. *Sufficient* for 3 or 4 persons. *Seasonable* at any time.

FRUIT, to Bottle Fresh. (Very useful in Winter.)

Ingredients.—Fresh fruits, such as currants, raspberries, cherries, gooseberries, plums of all kinds, damsons, &c.; wide-mouthed glass bottles, new corks to fit them tightly. *Mode.*—Let the fruit be full grown, but not too ripe, and gathered in dry weather. Pick it off the stalks without bruising or breaking the skin, and reject any that is at all blemished: if gathered in the damp, or if the skins are cut at all, the fruit will mould. Have ready some *perfectly dry* glass bottles, and some nice *new* soft corks or bungs; burn a match in each bottle, to exhaust the air, and quickly place the fruit in to be preserved; gently cork the bottles, and put them in a very cool oven, where let them remain until the fruit has shrunk away a fourth part. Then take the bottles out; *do not open them*, but immediately beat the corks in tight, cut off the tops, and cover them with melted resin. If kept in a dry place, the fruit will remain good for months; and on this principally depends the success of the preparation; for if stored away in a place that is in the least damp, the fruit will soon spoil. *Time.*—From 5 to 6 hours in a very slow oven.

FRUIT, to Bottle Fresh.

Ingredients.—Any kind of fresh fruit, such as currants, cherries, gooseberries, all kinds of plums, &c.; wide-mouthed glass bottles, new corks to fit them tightly. *Mode.*—the fruit must be full-grown, not too ripe, and gathered on a fine day. Let it be carefully picked and put into the bottles, which must be clean and perfectly dry. Tie over the tops of the bottles pieces of bladder; stand the bottles in a large pot, copper, or boiler, with cold water to reach to their necks; kindle a fire under, let the water boil, and as the bladders begin to rise and puff, prick them. As soon as the water boils, extinguish the fire, and let the bottles remain where they are, to become cold. The next day remove the bladders, and strew over the fruit a thick layer of pounded sugar; fit the bottles with cork, and let each cork lie close at hand to its own bottle. Hold for a few moments, in the neck of the bottle, two or three lighted matches, and when they have filled the bottle neck with gas, and before they go out, remove them very quickly; instantly cork the bottle closely, and dip it in bottle-cement. *Time.*—Altogether about 8 hours.

FRUIT, to Bottle Fresh, with Sugar. (Very useful in Winter.)

Ingredients.—Any kind of fresh fruit; to each quart bottle allow ¼ lb. of pounded sugar. *Mode.*—Let the fruit be gathered in dry weather. Pick it carefully, and drop it into *clean* and *very dry* quart glass bottles, sprinkling over it the above proportion of pounded sugar to each quart. Put the corks in the bottles, and place them in a copper of cold water up to their necks, with small hay-wisps round them, to prevent the bottles from knocking together. Light the fire under, bring the water gradually to boil, and let it simmer gently until the fruit in the bottles is reduced nearly one third. Extinguish the fire, *and let the bottles remain in the water until it is perfectly cold*; then take them out, make the corks secure, and cover them with melted resin or wax. *Time.*—About ½ hour from the time the water commences to boil.

FRUIT TURNOVERS (suitable for Pic-Nics).

Ingredients.—Puff-paste, any kind of fruit, sugar to taste. *Mode.*—Make some puff-paste by recipe; roll it out to the thickness of about ¼ inch, and cut it out in pieces of a circular form; pile the fruit on half of the paste, sprinkle over some sugar, wet the edges and turn the paste over. Press the edges together, ornament them, and brush the turnovers over with the white of an egg; sprinkle over sifted sugar, and bake on tins, in a brisk oven, for about 20 minutes. Instead of putting the fruit in raw, it may be boiled down with a little sugar first, and then inclosed in the crust; or jam, of any kind, may be substituted for fresh fruit. *Time.*—20 minutes. *Sufficient.*—½ lb. of puff-paste will make a dozen turnovers. *Seasonable* at any time.

GAME, Hashed.

[COLD MEAT COOKERY.] *Ingredients.*—The remains of cold game, 1 onion stuck with 3 cloves, a few whole peppers, a strip of lemon-peel, salt to taste, thickening of butter and flour, 1 glass of port wine, 1 tablespoonful of lemon-juice, 1 tablespoonful of ketchup, 1 pint of water or weak stock. *Mode.*—Cut the remains of cold game into joints, reserve the best pieces, and the inferior ones and trimmings put into a stewpan with the onion, pepper, lemon-peel, salt, and water or weak stock; stew these for about an hour, and strain the gravy; thicken it with butter and flour; add the wine, lemon-juice, and ketchup; lay in the pieces of game, and let them gradually warm through by the side of the fire; do not allow it to boil, or the game will be hard. When on the point of simmering, serve, and garnish the dish with sippets of toasted bread. *Time.*—Altogether 1¼ hour. *Seasonable* from August to March.

Note.—Any kind of game may be hashed by the above recipe, and the flavour may be varied by adding flavoured vinegars, curry powder, &c.; but we cannot recommend these latter ingredients, as a dish of game should really have a gamy taste; and if too many sauces, essences, &c., are added to the gravy, they quite overpower and destroy the flavour the dish should possess.

GERMAN PUFFS.

Ingredients.—2 oz. of flour, 2 eggs, ½ pint of new milk, 2 oz. of melted butter, little salt and nutmeg. *Mode.*—Let the 2 eggs be well beaten, then mix all the ingredients well together, and heat them up just before they are put into little cups half full for baking. Bake for ¼ hour in a hot oven till the puffs are of a nice brown; turn out on a flat dish, rub a little butter over each puff, and dust on it powdered sugar. *Time.*—¼ hour. *Average cost*, 6*d*. *Seasonable* at any time.

GHERKINS, Pickled.

Ingredients.—Salt and water, 1 oz. of bruised ginger ½ oz. of whole black pepper, ¼ oz. of whole allspice, 4 cloves, 2 blades of mace, a little horseradish. This proportion of pepper, spices, &c., for 1 quart of vinegar. *Mode.*—Let the gherkins remain in salt and water for 3 or 4 days, when take them out, wipe perfectly dry, and put them into a stone jar. Boil sufficient vinegar to cover them, with spices and pepper, &c., in the above proportion, for 10 minutes; pour it, quite boiling, over the gherkins, cover the jar with vine-leaves, and put over them a plate, setting them near the fire, where they must remain all night. Next day drain off the vinegar, boil it up again, and pour it hot over them. Cover up with fresh leaves, and let the whole remain till quite cold. Now tie down closely with bladder to exclude the air, and in a month or two they will be fit for use. *Time.*—4 days. *Seasonable* from the middle of July to the end of August.

GIBLET PIE.

Ingredients.—A set of duck or goose giblets, 1 lb. of rump-steak, 1 onion, ½ teaspoonful of whole black pepper, a bunch of savoury herbs, plain crust. *Mode.*—Clean, and put the giblets into a stewpan with an onion, whole pepper, and a bunch of savoury herbs; add rather more than a pint of water, and simmer gently for about 1½ hour. Take them out, let them cool, and cut them into pieces; line the bottom of a pie-dish with a few pieces of rump-steak; add a layer of giblets and a few more pieces of steak; season with pepper and salt, and pour in the gravy (which should be strained), that the giblets were stewed in; cover with a plain crust, and bake for rather more than 1½ hour in a brisk oven. Cover a piece of paper over the pie, to prevent the crust taking too much colour. *Time.*—1½ hour to stew the giblets, about 1 hour to bake the pie. *Average cost*, exclusive of the giblets, 1*s*. 4*d*. *Sufficient* for 5 or 6 persons.

GIBLET SOUP.

Ingredients.—3 sets of goose or duck giblets, 2 lbs. of shin of beef, a few bones, 1 ox-tail, 2 mutton-shanks, 2 large onions, 2 carrots, 1 large faggot of herbs, salt and pepper to taste, ¼ pint of cream, 1 oz. of butter mixed with a dessertspoonful of flour, 3 quarts of water. *Mode.*—Scald the giblets, cut the gizzards in 8 pieces, and put them in a stewpan with the beef, bones, ox-tail, mutton-shanks, onions, herbs, pepper, and salt; add the 3 quarts of water, and simmer till the giblets are tender, taking care to skim well. When the giblets are done, take them out, put them in your tureen, strain the soup through a sieve, add the cream and butter, mixed with a dessertspoonful of flour, boil it up for a few minutes, and pour it over the giblets. It can be flavoured with port wine and a little mushroom ketchup, instead of cream. Add salt to taste. *Time.*—3 hours. *Average cost*, 9*d*. per quart. *Seasonable* all the year. *Sufficient* for 10 persons.

GINGER, Apple. (A Dessert Dish.)

Ingredients.—2 lbs. of any kind of hard apples, 2 lbs. of loaf sugar, 1½ pint of water, 1 oz. of tincture of ginger. *Mode.*—Boil the sugar and water until they form a rich syrup, adding the ginger when it boils up. Pare, core, and cut the apples into pieces; dip them in cold water to preserve the colour, and boil them in the syrup until transparent; but be careful not to let them break. Put the pieces of apple into jars, pour over the syrup, and carefully exclude the air, by well covering them. It will remain good some time, if kept in a dry place. *Time.*—From 5 to 10 minutes to boil the syrup; about ½ hour to simmer the apples. *Average cost,* 2s. *Sufficient* for 7 or 8 persons. *Seasonable.*—Make this in September, October, or November.

GINGER-BEER.

Ingredients.—2½ lbs. of loaf sugar, 1½ oz. of bruised ginger, 1 oz. of cream of tartar, the rind and juice of 2 lemons, 3 gallons of boiling water, two large tablespoonfuls of thick and fresh brewer's yeast. *Mode.*—Peel the lemons, squeeze the juice, strain it, and put the peel and juice into a large earthen pan, with the bruised ginger, cream of tartar, and loaf sugar. Put over these ingredients 3 gallons of *boiling* water; let it stand until just warm, when add the yeast, which should be thick and perfectly fresh. Stir the contents of the pan well, and let them remain near the fire all night, covering the pan over with a cloth. The next day skim off the yeast, and pour the liquor carefully into another vessel, leaving the sediment; then bottle immediately, and tie the corks down, and in 3 days the ginger-beer will be fit for use. For some tastes, the above proportion of sugar may be found rather too large, when it may be diminished; but the beer will not keep so long good. *Average cost* for this quantity, 2s.; or ½d. per bottle. *Sufficient* to fill 4 dozen ginger-beer bottles. *Seasonable.*—This should be made during the summer months.

GINGER CREAM.

Ingredients.—The yolks of 4 eggs, 1 pint of cream, 3 oz. of preserved ginger, 2 dessertspoonfuls of syrup, sifted sugar to taste, 1 oz. of isinglass. *Mode.*—Slice the ginger finely; put it into a basin with the syrup, the well-beaten yolks of eggs, and the cream; mix these ingredients well together, and stir them over the fire for about 10 minutes, or until the mixture thickens; then take it off the fire, whisk till nearly cold, sweeten to taste, add the isinglass, which should be melted and strained, and serve the cream in a glass dish. It may be garnished with slices of preserved ginger or candied citron. *Time.*—About 10 minutes to stir the cream over the fire. *Average cost,* with cream at 1*s.* per pint, 3*s.* 6*d. Sufficient* for a good-sized dish. *Seasonable* at any time.

GINGER, Preserved,

Comes from the West Indies. It is made by scalding the roots when they are green and full of sap, then peeling them in cold water and putting them into jars, with a rich syrup; in which state we receive them. It should be chosen of a deep yellow colour, with a little transparency. What is dark-coloured, fibrous, and stringy, is not good. Ginger roots, fit for preserving and in size equal to West Indian, have been produced in the Royal Agricultural Garden in Edinburgh.

GINGER PUDDING.

Ingredients.—½ lb. of flour, ¼ lb. of suet, ¼ lb. of moist sugar, 2 large teaspoonfuls of grated ginger. *Mode.*—Shred the suet very fine, mix it with the flour, sugar, and ginger; stir all well together; butter a basin, and put the mixture in dry; tie a cloth over, and boil for 3 hours. *Time.*—3 hours. *Average cost,* 6*d. Sufficient* for 5 or 6 persons. *Seasonable* at any time.

GINGER WINE.

Ingredients.—To 9 gallons of water allow 27 lbs. of loaf sugar, 9 lemons, 12 oz. of bruised ginger, 3 tablespoonfuls of yeast, 2 lbs. of raisins stoned and chopped, 1 pint of brandy. *Mode.*—Boil together for 1 hour in a copper (let it previously be well scoured and beautifully clean) the water, sugar, *lemon-rinds,* and bruised ginger; remove every particle of scum as it rises, and when the liquor is sufficiently boiled, put it into a large tub or pan, as it must not remain in the copper. When nearly cold, add the yeast, which must be thick and very fresh, and, the next day, put all in a dry cask with the strained lemon-juice and chopped raisins. Stir the wine every day for a fortnight; then add the brandy, stop the cask down by degrees, and in a few weeks it will be fit to bottle. *Average cost,* 2*s.* per gallon. *Sufficient* to make 9 gallons of wine. *Seasonable.*—The best time for making this wine is either in March or September.

Note.—Wine made early in March will be fit to bottle in June.

GINGERBREAD, Thick.

Ingredients.—1 lb. of treacle, ¼ lb. of butter, ¼ lb. of coarse brown sugar, 1½ lb. of flour, 1 oz. of ginger, ½ oz. of ground allspice, 1 teaspoonful of carbonate of soda, ¼ pint of warm milk, 3 eggs. *Mode.*—Put the flour into a basin, with the sugar, ginger, and allspice; mix these together; warm the butter, and add it, with the treacle, to the other ingredients. Stir well; make the milk just warm, dissolve the carbonate of soda in it, and mix the whole into a nice smooth dough with the eggs, which should be previously well whisked; pour the mixture into a buttered tin, and bake it from ¾ to 1 hour, or longer, should the gingerbread be very thick. Just before it is done, brush the top over with the yolk of an egg beaten up with a little milk, and put it back in the oven to finish baking. *Time.*—¾ to 1 hour. *Average cost*, 1*s.* per square. *Seasonable* at any time.

GINGERBREAD, White.

Ingredients.—1 lb. of flour, ½ lb. of butter, ½ lb. of loaf sugar, the rind of 1 lemon, 1 oz. of ground ginger, 1 nutmeg grated, ½ teaspoonful of carbonate of soda, 1 gill of milk. *Mode.*—Rub the butter into the flour; add the sugar, which should be finely pounded and sifted, and the minced lemon-rind, ginger, and nutmeg. Mix these well together; make the milk just warm, stir in the soda, and work the whole into a nice smooth paste; roll it out, cut it into cakes, and bake in a moderate oven from 15 to 20 minutes. *Time.*—15 to 20 minutes. *Average cost*, 1*s.* 3*d. Seasonable* at any time.

GINGERBREAD-NUTS, Rich Sweetmeats.

Ingredients.—1 lb. of treacle, ¼ lb. of clarified butter, 1 lb. of coarse brown sugar, 2 oz. of ground ginger, 1 oz. of candied orange-peel, 1 oz. of candied angelica, ½ oz. of candied lemon-peel, ½ oz. of coriander seeds, ½ oz. of caraway seeds, 1 egg; flour. *Mode.*—Put the treacle into a basin, and pour over it the butter, melted so as not to oil, the sugar, and ginger. Stir these ingredients well together, and whilst mixing, add the candied peel, which should be cut into very small pieces, but not bruised, and the caraway and coriander seeds, which should be pounded. Having mixed all thoroughly together, break in an egg, and work the whole up with as much fine flour as may be necessary to form a paste. Make this into nuts of any size, and put them on a tin plate, and bake in a slow oven from ¼ to ½ hour. *Time.*—¼ to ½ hour. *Average cost*, from 1*s*. to 1*s*. 4*d*. per lb. *Seasonable* at any time.

GINGERBREAD-NUTS, Sunderland. (An Excellent Recipe.)

Ingredients.—1¾ lb. of treacle, 1 lb. of moist sugar, 1 lb. of butter, 2¾ lbs. of flour, 1½ oz. of ground ginger, 1½ oz. of allspice, 1½ oz. of coriander-seeds. *Mode.*—Let the allspice, coriander-seeds, and ginger be freshly ground; put them into a basin, with the flour and sugar, and mix these ingredients well together; warm the treacle and butter together; then with a spoon work it into the flour, &c. until the whole forms a nice smooth paste. Drop the mixture from the spoon on a piece of buttered paper, and bake in rather a slow oven from 20 minutes to ½ hour. A little candied lemon-peel mixed with the above is an improvement, and a great authority in culinary matters suggests the addition of a little cayenne pepper in gingerbread. Whether it be advisable to use the latter ingredient or not, we leave our readers to decide. *Time.*—20 minutes to ½ hour. *Average cost*, 1*s*. to 1*s*. 4*d*. per lb. *Seasonable* at any time.

GLAZE for covering Cold Hams, Tongues, &c.

Ingredients.—Stock, doubling the quantity of meat in the recipes. *Mode.* —We may remark at the outset, that unless glaze is wanted in very large quantities, it is seldom made expressly. Either of the stocks, boiled down and reduced very considerably, will be found to produce a very good glaze. Put the stock into a stewpan, over a nice clear fire; let it boil till it becomes somewhat stiff, when keep stirring, to prevent its burning. The moment it is sufficiently reduced, and come to a glaze, turn it into the glaze-pot before it gets cold. As, however, this is not to be found in every establishment, a white earthenware jar would answer the purpose; and this may be placed in a vessel of boiling water, to melt the glaze when required. It should never be warmed in a saucepan, except on the principle of the bain marie, lest it should reduce too much, and become black and bitter. If the glaze is wanted of a pale colour, more veal than beef should be used in making the stock; and it is as well to omit turnips and celery, as those impart a disagreeable bitter flavour.

GLAZE-KETTLE.

GLAZE-KETTLE.

This is a kettle used for keeping the strong stock boiled down to a jelly, which is known by the name of glaze. It is composed of two tin vessels, as shown in the cut, one of which, the upper,—containing the glaze, is inserted into one of larger diameter, and containing boiling water.

GLAZE, to, Cold Joints, &c.

Melt the glaze by placing the vessel which contains it, into the bain marie or saucepan of boiling water; brush it over the meat with a paste-brush, and if in places it is not quite covered, repeat the operation. The glaze should not be too dark a colour.

GOLDEN PUDDING.

Ingredients.—¼ lb. of bread-crumbs, ¼ lb. of suet, ¼ lb. of marmalade, ¼ lb. of sugar, 4 eggs. *Mode.*—Put the bread-crumbs into a basin; mix with them the suet, which should be finely minced, the marmalade, and the sugar; stir all these ingredients well together, beat the eggs to a froth, moisten the pudding with these, and when well mixed put it into a mould or buttered basin; tie down with a floured cloth, and boil for 2 hours. When turned out, strew a little fine-sifted sugar over the top, and serve. *Time.*—2 hours. *Average cost*, 11*d*. *Sufficient* for 5 or 6 persons. *Seasonable* at any time.

Note.—The mould may be ornamented with stoned raisins, arranged in any fanciful pattern, before the mixture is poured in, which would add very much to the appearance of the pudding. For a plainer pudding, double the quantities of the bread-crumbs; and if the eggs do not moisten it sufficiently, use a little milk.

GOOSE, Green.

Ingredients.—Goose, 3 oz. of butter, pepper and salt to taste. *Mode.*—Geese are called green till they are about four months old, and should not be stuffed. After it has been singed and trussed, put into the body a seasoning of pepper and salt, and the butter to moisten it inside. Roast before a clear fire for about ¾ hour, froth and brown it nicely, and serve with a brown gravy, and, when liked, gooseberry-sauce. This dish should be garnished with water-cresses. *Time.*—About ¾ hour. *Average cost*, 4*s.* 6*d.* each. *Sufficient* for 5 or 6 persons. *Seasonable* in June, July, and August.

GOOSE, Hashed.

[COLD MEAT COOKERY.] *Ingredients.*—The remains of cold roast goose, 2 onions, 2 oz. of butter, 1 pint of boiling water, 1 dessertspoonful of flour, pepper and salt to taste, 1 tablespoonful of port wine, 2 tablespoonfuls of mushroom ketchup. *Mode.*—Cut up the goose into pieces of the size required; the inferior joints, trimmings, &c., put into a stewpan to make the gravy; slice and fry the onions in the butter of a very pale brown; add these to the trimmings, and pour over about a pint of boiling water; stew these gently for ¾ hour, then skim and strain the liquor. Thicken it with flour, and flavour with port wine and ketchup in the above proportion; add a seasoning of pepper and salt, and put in the pieces of goose; let these get thoroughly hot through, but do not allow them to boil, and serve with sippets of toasted bread. *Time.*—Altogether, rather more than 1 hour. *Average cost*, exclusive of the cold goose, 4*d. Seasonable* from September to March.

GOOSE, Roast.

ROAST GOOSE.

Ingredients.—Goose, 4 large onions, 10 sage-leaves, ¼ lb. of bread-crumbs, 1½ oz. of butter, salt and pepper to taste, 1 egg. *Choosing and Trussing.*—Select a goose with a clean white skin, plump breast, and yellow feet: if these latter are red, the bird is old. Should the weather permit, let it hang for a few days; by so doing the flavour will be very much improved. Pluck, singe, draw, and carefully wash and wipe the goose; cut off the neck close to the back, leaving the skin long enough to turn over; cut off the feet at the first joint, and separate the pinions at the first joint. Beat the breastbone flat with a rolling-pin, put a skewer through the under part of each wing, and having drawn up the legs closely, put a skewer into the middle of each, and pass the same quite through the body. Insert another skewer into the small of the leg, bring it close down to the side-bone, run it through, and do the same to the other side. Now cut off the end of the vent, and make a hole in the skin sufficiently large for the passage of the rump, in order to keep in the seasoning. *Mode.*—Make a sage-and-onion stuffing of the above ingredients, put it into the body of the goose, and secure it firmly at both ends by passing the rump through the hole made in the skin, and the other end by tying the skin of the neck to the back: by this means the seasoning will not escape. Put it down to a brisk fire, keep it well basted, and roast from 1½ to 2 hours, according to the size. Remove the skewers, and serve with a tureen of good gravy, and one of well-made apple sauce. Should a very highly-flavoured seasoning be preferred, the onions should not be parboiled, but minced raw: of the two methods the mild seasoning is far superior. A ragoût, or pie, should be made of the giblets, or they may be stewed down to make gravy. Be careful to serve the goose before the breast falls, or its appearance will be spoiled by coming flattened to table. As this is rather a troublesome joint to carve, a *large* quantity of gravy should not be poured round the goose, but sent in a tureen. *Time.*—A large goose, 1¾ hour; a moderate-sized one, 1/¼ to 1½ hour. *Seasonable* from September to March; but in perfection from Michaelmas to Christmas. *Average cost*, 5s. 6d. each. *Sufficient* for 8 or 9 persons.

Note.—A teaspoonful of made mustard, a saltspoonful of salt, a few grains of cayenne, mixed with a glass of port wine, are sometimes poured into the goose by a slit made in the apron. This sauce is by many considered an improvement.

GOOSE, Roast, to Carve.

ROAST GOOSE.

LEG, WING, AND NECK-BONE OF GOOSE.

It would not be fair to say that this dish bodes a great deal of happiness to an inexperienced carver, especially if there is a large party to serve, and the slices off the breast should not suffice to satisfy the desires and cravings of many wholesome appetites, produced, may be, by the various sports in vogue at Michaelmas and Christmas. The beginning of the task, however, is not in any way difficult. Evenly-cut slices, not too thick or too thin, should be carved from the breast in the direction of the line from 2 to 3; after the first slice has been cut, a hole should be made with the knife in the part called the apron, passing it round the line as indicated by the figures 1, 1, 1; here the stuffing is located, and some of this should be served on each plate, unless it is discovered that it is not agreeable to the taste of some one guest. If the carver manages cleverly, he will be able to cut a very large number of fine slices off the breast, and the more so if he commences close down by the wing, and carves upwards towards the ridge of the breastbone. As many slices as can be taken from the breast being carved, the wings should be cut off, and the same process as described in carving boiled fowl is made use of in this instance, only more dexterity and greater force will most probably be required. The shape of the leg, when disengaged from the body of the goose, should be like that shown in the accompanying engraving. It will be necessary, perhaps, in taking off the leg, to turn the goose on its side, and then, pressing down the small end of the leg, the knife should be passed under it from the top quite down to the joint; the leg being now turned back by the fork, the knife must cut through the joint, loosening the thighbone from its socket. The merrythought, which in a goose is not so large as might be expected, is disengaged in the same way as that of a fowl—by passing the knife under it, and pressing it backwards towards the neck. The neck-bones, of which we give a cut, are freed by the same process as are those of a fowl; and the same may be said of all the other parts of this bird. The breast of a goose is the part most esteemed; all parts, however, are good, and full of juicy flavour.

GOOSE STUFFING, Soyer's Recipe for.

Take 4 apples peeled and cored, 4 onions, 4 leaves of sage, and 4 leaves of lemon thyme not broken, and boil them in a stewpan with sufficient water to cover them; when done, pulp them through a sieve, removing the sage and thyme; then add sufficient pulp of mealy potatoes to cause it to be sufficiently dry without sticking to the hand; add pepper and salt, and stuff the bird.

GOOSEBERRIES, Compôte of.

Ingredients.—Syrup; to 1 pint of syrup allow nearly a quart of gooseberries. *Mode.*—Top and tail the gooseberries, which should not be very ripe, and pour over them some boiling water; then take them out and plunge them into cold water with which has been mixed a tablespoonful of vinegar, which will assist to keep the fruit a good colour. Make a pint of syrup, and when it boils drain the gooseberries and put them in; simmer them gently until the fruit is nicely pulped and tender without being broken; then dish the gooseberries on a glass dish, boil the syrup for 2 or 3 minutes, pour over the gooseberries, and serve cold. *Time.*—About 5 minutes to boil the gooseberries in the syrup, 3 minutes to reduce the syrup. *Average cost*,

9*d*. *Sufficient.*—A quart of gooseberries for 5 or 6 persons. *Seasonable* in June.

GOOSEBERRY CHIPS. (Useful for Dessert.)

Ingredients.—Gooseberries unripe and green, but quite full-grown; sifted loaf sugar. *Mode.*—Put the gooseberries, when cleaned of tops and tails, into jars, and boil them in a copper till quite soft. To every lb. of pulp put ½ lb. of loaf sugar sifted: the sugar must be stirred in very gently. Then pour out the sweetened pulp on flat dishes, about ⅛ inch thick, which must be set in the sun to dry. When sufficiently dried in the sun, the pulp may be cut into strips, and twisted into any fanciful shapes, bows, &c. *Time* for drying, according to the amount of sun. *Seasonable* at all times.

Note.—These chips may be kept for years in tin boxes, if packed quite dry, with layers of paper between the rows.

GOOSEBERRY FOOL.

Ingredients.—Green gooseberries; to every pint of pulp add 1 pint of milk, or ½ pint of cream and ½ pint of milk; sugar to taste. *Mode.*—Cut the tops and tails off the gooseberries, put them into a jar with 2 tablespoonfuls of water and a little good moist sugar; set this jar in a saucepan of boiling water, and let it boil until the fruit is soft enough to mash. When done enough, beat it to a pulp, work this pulp through a colander, and stir to every pint the above proportion of milk, or equal quantities of milk and cream. Ascertain if the mixture is sweet enough, and put in plenty of sugar, or it will not be eatable; and in mixing the milk and gooseberries add the former very gradually to these: serve in a glass dish, or in small glasses. This, although a very old-fashioned and homely dish, is, when well made, very delicious, and, if properly sweetened, a very suitable preparation for children. *Time.*—From ¾ to 1 hour. *Average cost,* 6*d*. per pint, with milk. *Sufficient.*—A pint of milk and a pint of gooseberry pulp for 5 or 6 children. *Seasonable* in May and June.

GOOSEBERRY JAM.

Ingredients.—To every lb. of fruit allow ¾ lb. of loaf sugar; currant-juice. *Mode.*—Select red hairy gooseberries; have them gathered in dry weather, when quite ripe, without being too soft. Weigh them; with a pair of scissors cut off the tops and tails, and to every 6 lbs. of fruit have ready ½ pint of red-currant juice, drawn as for jelly. Put the gooseberries and currant-juice into a preserving-pan, let them boil tolerably quickly, keeping them well stirred; when they begin to break, add to them the sugar, and keep simmering until the jam becomes firm, carefully skimming and stirring it, that it does not burn at the bottom. It should be boiled rather a long time, or it will not keep. Put it into pots (not too large), let it get perfectly cold, then cover the pots down with oiled and egged papers. *Time.*—About 1 hour to boil the gooseberries in the currant-juice, from ½ to ¾ hour with the sugar. *Average cost*, per lb. pot, from 6*d.* to 8*d.* *Sufficient.*—Allow 1½ pint of fruit for a lb. pot. *Seasonable.*—Make this in June or July.

GOOSEBERRY JAM.

Ingredients.—To every 8 lbs. of red, rough, ripe gooseberries allow 1 quart of red-currant juice, 5 lbs. of loaf sugar. *Mode.*—Have the fruit gathered in dry weather, and cut off the tops and tails. Prepare 1 quart of red-currant juice, the same as for red-currant jelly; put it into a preserving-pan with the sugar, and keep stirring until the latter is dissolved. Keep it boiling for about 5 minutes; skim well; then put in the gooseberries, and let them boil from ½ to ¾ hour; then turn the whole into an earthen pan, and let it remain for 2 days. Boil the jam up again until it looks clear; put it into pots, and when cold, cover with oiled paper, and over the jars put tissue-paper brushed over on both sides with the white of an egg, and store away in a dry place. Care must be taken, in making this, to keep the jam well stirred and well skimmed, to prevent it burning at the bottom of the pan, and to have it very clear. *Time.*—5 minutes to boil the currant-juice and sugar after the latter is dissolved; from ½ to ¾ hour to simmer the gooseberries the first time, ¼ hour the second time of boiling. *Average cost*, from 8*d.* to 10*d.* per lb. pot. *Sufficient.*—Allow 1½ pint of fruit for a lb. pot. *Seasonable.*—Make this in June or July.

GOOSEBERRY JAM, White or Green.

Ingredients.—Equal weight of fruit and sugar. *Mode.*—Select the gooseberries not very ripe, either white or green, and top and tail them. Boil the sugar with water (allowing ½ pint to every lb.) for about ¼ hour, carefully removing the scum as it rises; then put in the gooseberries, and simmer gently till clear and firm: try a little of the jam on a plate; if it jellies when cold, it is done, and should then be poured into pots. When cold, cover with oiled paper, and tissue-paper brushed over on both sides with the unbeaten white of an egg, and stow away in a dry place. *Time.*—¼ hour to boil the sugar and water, ¾ hour the jam. *Average cost*, from 6*d.* to 8*d.* per lb. pot. *Sufficient.*—Allow 1½ pint of fruit for a lb. pot. *Seasonable.*—Make this in June.

GOOSEBERRY JELLY.

Ingredients.—Gooseberries; to every pint of juice allow ¾ lb. of loaf sugar. *Mode.*—Put the gooseberries, after cutting off the tops and tails, into a preserving-pan, and stir them over the fire until they are quite soft; then strain them through a sieve, and to every pint of juice allow ¾ lb. of sugar. Boil the juice and sugar together for nearly ¾ hour, stirring and skimming all the time; and if the jelly appears firm when a little of it is poured on to a plate, it is done, and should then be taken up and put into small pots. Cover the pots with oiled and egged papers, the same as for currant jelly, and store away in a dry place. *Time.*—¾ hour to simmer the gooseberries without the sugar; ¾ hour to boil the juice. *Average cost*, from 8*d.* to 10*d.* per ½-lb. pot. *Seasonable* in July.

GOOSEBERRY PUDDING, Baked.

Ingredients.—Gooseberries, 3 eggs, 1½ oz. of butter, ½ pint of bread-crumbs, sugar to taste. *Mode.*—Put the gooseberries into a jar, previously cutting off the tops and tails; place this jar in boiling water, and let it boil until the gooseberries are soft enough to pulp; then beat them through a coarse sieve, and to every pint of pulp add 3 well-whisked eggs, 1½ oz. of butter, ½ pint of bread-crumbs, and sugar to taste; beat the mixture well, put a border of puff-paste round the edge of a pie-dish, put in the pudding, bake for about 40 minutes, strew sifted sugar over, and serve. *Time.*—About 40 minutes. *Average cost*, 10*d*. *Sufficient* for 4 or 5 persons. *Seasonable* from May to July.

GOOSEBERRY PUDDING, Boiled.

BOILED FRUIT PUDDING

Ingredients.—¾ lb. of suet crust, 1½ pint of green gooseberries, ¼ lb. of moist sugar. *Mode.*—Line a pudding-basin with suet crust rolled out to about ½ inch in thickness, and, with a pair of scissors, cut off the tops and tails of the gooseberries; fill the basin with the fruit, put in the sugar, and cover with crust. Pinch the edges of the pudding together, tie over it a floured cloth, put it into boiling water, and boil from 2½ to 3 hours; turn it out of the basin, and serve with a jug of cream. *Time.*—2½ to 3 hours. *Average cost*, 10*d*. *Sufficient* for 6 or 7 persons. *Seasonable* from May to July.

GOOSEBERRY SAUCE for Boiled Mackerel.

Ingredients.—1 pint of green gooseberries, 3 tablespoonfuls of Béchamel (veal gravy may be substituted for this), 2 oz. of fresh butter; seasoning to taste of salt, pepper, and grated nutmeg. *Mode.*—Boil the gooseberries in water until quite tender; strain them, and rub them through a sieve. Put into a saucepan the Béchamel or gravy, with the butter and seasoning; add the pulp from the gooseberries, mix all well together, and heat gradually through. A little pounded sugar added to this sauce is by many persons considered an improvement, as the saccharine matter takes off the extreme acidity of the unripe fruit. *Time.*—Boil the gooseberries from 20 minutes to ½ hour. *Sufficient.*—This quantity, for a large dish of mackerel. *Seasonable* from May to July.

GOOSEBERRY TART.

Ingredients.—1½ pint of gooseberries, ½ lb. of short crust, ¼ lb. of moist sugar. *Mode.*—With a pair of scissors cut off the tops and tails of the gooseberries; put them into a deep pie-dish, pile the fruit high in the centre, and put in the sugar; line the edge of the dish with short crust, put on the cover, and ornament the edges of the tart; bake in a good oven for about ¾ hour, and before being sent to table, strew over it some fine-sifted sugar. A jug of cream, or a dish of boiled or baked custards, should always accompany this dish. *Time.*—¾ hour. *Average cost,* 9*d*. *Sufficient* for 5 or 6 persons. *Seasonable* from May to July.

GOOSEBERRY TRIFLE.

Ingredients.—1 quart of gooseberries, sugar to taste, 1 pint of custard, a plateful of whipped cream. *Mode.*—Put the gooseberries into a jar, with sufficient moist sugar to sweeten them, and boil them until reduced to a pulp. Put this pulp at the bottom of a trifle-dish; pour over it a pint of custard made by recipe, and, when cold, cover with whipped cream. The cream should be whipped the day before it is wanted for table, as it will then be so much firmer and more solid; but it should not be added to the fruit until a short time before it is required. The dish may be garnished as fancy dictates. *Time.*—About ¾ hour to boil the gooseberries. *Average cost,* 1*s*. 6*d*. *Sufficient* for 1 trifle. *Seasonable* in May, June, and July.

GOOSEBERRY VINEGAR. (An Excellent Recipe.)

Ingredients.—2 pecks of crystal gooseberries, 6 gallons of water, 12 lbs. of foots sugar of the coarsest brown quality. *Mode.*—Mash the gooseberries (which should be quite ripe) in a tub with a mallet; put to them the water nearly milk-warm; let this stand 24 hours; then strain it through a sieve, and put the sugar to it; mix it well, and tun it. These proportions are for a 9-gallon cask; and if it be not quite full, more water must be added. Let the mixture be stirred from the bottom of the cask two or three times daily for three or four days, to assist the melting of the sugar; then paste a piece of linen cloth over the bunghole, and set the cask in a warm place, *but not in the sun*; any corner of a warm kitchen is the best situation for it. The following spring it should be drawn off into stone bottles, and the vinegar will be fit for use twelve months after it is made. This will be found a most excellent preparation, greatly superior to much that is sold under the name of the best white wine vinegar. Many years' experience has proved that pickle made with this vinegar will keep, when bought vinegar will not preserve the ingredients. The cost per gallon is merely nominal, especially to those who reside in the country and grow their own gooseberries; the coarse sugar is then the only ingredient to be purchased. *Time.*—To remain in the cask 9 months. *Average cost*, when the gooseberries have to be purchased, 1*s.* per gallon; when they are grown at home, 6*d.* per gallon. *Seasonable.*—This should be made the end of June or the beginning of July, when gooseberries are ripe and plentiful.

GOOSEBERRY WINE, Effervescing.

Ingredients.—To every gallon of water allow 6 lbs. of green gooseberries, 3 lbs. of lump sugar. *Mode.*—This wine should be prepared from unripe gooseberries, in order to avoid the flavour which the fruit would give to the wine when in a mature state. Its briskness depends more upon the time of bottling than upon the unripe state of the fruit, for effervescing wine can be made from fruit that is ripe as well as that which is unripe. The fruit should be selected when it has nearly attained its full growth, and consequently before it shows any tendency to ripen. Any bruised or decayed berries, and those that are very small, should be rejected. The blossom and stalk ends should be removed, and the fruit well bruised in a tub or pan, in such quantities as to insure each berry being broken without crushing the seeds. Pour the water (which should be warm) on the fruit, squeeze and stir it with the hand until all the pulp is removed from the skin and seeds, and cover the whole closely for 24 hours; after which, strain it through a coarse bag, and press it with as much force as can be conveniently applied, to extract the whole of the juice and liquor the fruit may contain. To every 40 or 50 lbs. of fruit one gallon more of hot water may be passed through the *marc*, or husks, in order to obtain any soluble matter that may remain, and be again pressed. The juice should be put into a tub or pan of sufficient size to contain all of it, and the sugar added to it. Let it be well stirred until the sugar is dissolved, and place the pan in a warm situation; keep it closely covered, and let it ferment for a day or two. It must then be drawn off into clean casks, placed a little on one side for the scum that arises to be thrown out, and the casks kept filled with the remaining "must," that should be reserved for that purpose. When the active fermentation has ceased, the casks should be plugged upright, again filled, if necessary, the bungs be put in loosely, and, after a few days, when the fermentation is a little more languid (which may be known by the hissing noise ceasing), the bungs should be driven in tight, and a spile-hole made, to give vent if necessary. About November or December, on a clear fine day, the wine should be racked from its lees into clean casks, which may be rinsed with brandy. After a month, it should be examined to see if it is sufficiently clear for bottling; if not, it must be fined with isinglass, which may be dissolved in some of the wine: 1 oz. will be sufficient for 9 gallons. In bottling the wine, it will be necessary to wire the corks down, or to tie them down with string. Old champagne bottles are the best for this wine. In March or April, or when the gooseberry bushes begin to blossom, the wine must be bottled, in order to insure its being effervescing. *Seasonable.—* Make this the end of May or beginning of June, before the berries ripen.

GRAVIES, General Stock for

By the addition of various store sauces, thickening and flavouring, good stock may be converted into good gravies. It should be borne in mind, however, that the goodness and strength of spices, wines, flavourings, &c., evaporate, and that they lose a great deal of their fragrance if added to the gravy a long time before they are wanted. If this point is attended to, a saving of one half the quantity of these ingredients will be effected, as, with long boiling, the flavour almost entirely passes away. The shank-bones of mutton, previously well soaked, will be found a great assistance in enriching gravies; a kidney or melt, beef skirt, trimmings of meat, &c. &c., answer very well when only a small quantity is wanted, and a good gravy need not necessarily be so very expensive; for economically-prepared dishes are oftentimes found as savoury and wholesome as dearer ones. The cook should also remember that the fragrance of gravies should not be overpowered by too much spice, or any strong essences, and that they should always be warmed in a *bain marie*, after they are flavoured, or else in a jar or jug placed in a saucepan full of boiling water. The remains of roast-meat gravy should always be saved; as, when no meat is at hand, a very nice gravy in haste may be made from it, and when added to hashes, ragoûts, &c., is a great improvement.

GRAVY, a Good Beef, for Poultry, Game, &c.

Ingredients.—½ lb. of lean beef, ½ pint of cold water, 1 shalot or small onion, ½ a teaspoonful of salt, a little pepper, 1 tablespoonful of Harvey's sauce or mushroom ketchup, ½ a teaspoonful of arrowroot. *Mode.*—Cut up the beef into small pieces, and put it, with the water, into a stewpan. Add the shalot and seasoning, and simmer gently for 3 hours, taking care that it does not boil fast. A short time before it is required, take the arrowroot, and having mixed it with a little cold water, pour it into the gravy, which keep stirring, adding the Harvey's sauce, and just letting it boil. Strain off the gravy in a tureen, and serve very hot. *Time.*—3 hours. *Average cost*, 8*d.* per pint.

GRAVY, Beef, a Quickly Made.

Ingredients.—½ lb. of shin of beef, ½ onion, ¼ carrot, 2 or 3 sprigs of parsley and savoury herbs, a piece of butter about the size of a walnut; cayenne and mace to taste, ¾ pint of water. *Mode.*—Cut up the meat into very small pieces, slice the onion and carrot, and put them into a small saucepan with the butter. Keep stirring over a sharp fire until they have taken a little colour, when add the water and the remaining ingredients. Simmer for ½ hour, skim well, strain, and flavour, when it will be ready for use. *Time.*—½ hour. *Average cost*, for this quantity, 5*d.*

GRAVY, Brown.

Ingredients.—2 oz. of butter, 2 large onions, 2 lbs. of shin of beef, 2 small slices of lean bacon (if at hand), salt and whole pepper to taste, 3 cloves, 2 quarts of water. For thickening, 2 oz. of butter, 3 oz. of flour. *Mode.*—Put the butter into a stewpan; set this on the fire, throw in the onions cut in rings, and fry them a light brown; then add the beef and bacon, which should be cut into small square pieces; season, and pour in a teacupful of water; let it boil for about ten minutes, or until it is of a nice brown colour, occasionally stirring the contents. Now fill up with water in the above proportion; let it boil up, when draw it to the side of the fire to simmer very gently for 1½ hour; strain, and when cold, take off all the fat. In thickening this gravy, melt 3 oz. of butter in a stewpan, add 2 oz. of flour, and stir till of a light-brown colour; when cold, add it to the strained gravy, and boil it up quickly. This thickening may be made in larger quantities, and kept in a stone jar for use when wanted. *Time.*—Altogether, 2 hours. *Average cost*, 4*d*. per pint.

GRAVY, Brown, without Meat.

Ingredients.—2 large onions, 1 large carrot, 2 oz. of butter, 3 pints of boiling water, 1 bunch of savoury herbs, a wineglassful of good beer; salt and pepper to taste. *Mode.*—Slice, flour, and fry the onions and carrots in the butter until of a nice light-brown colour, then add the boiling water and the remaining ingredients; let the whole stew gently for about an hour, then strain, and when cold, skim off all the fat. Thicken it, and, if thought necessary, add a few drops of colouring. *Time.*—1 hour. *Average cost*, 2*d*. per pint.

Note.—The addition of a small quantity of mushroom ketchup or Harvey's sauce very much improves the flavour of this gravy.

GRAVY, Cheap, for Minced Veal

Ingredients.—Bones and trimmings of cold roast or boiled veal, 1½ pint of water, 1 onion, ¼ teaspoonful of minced lemon-peel, ¼ teaspoonful of salt, 1 blade of pounded mace, the juice of ¼ lemon; thickening of butter and flour. *Mode.*—Put all the ingredients into a stewpan, except the thickening and lemon-juice, and let them simmer very gently for rather more than 1 hour, or until the liquor is reduced to a pint, when strain through a hair sieve. Add a thickening of butter and flour, and the lemon-juice; set it on the fire, and let it just boil up, when it will be ready for use. It may be flavoured with a little tomato sauce, and, where a rather dark-coloured gravy is not objected to, ketchup, or Harvey's sauce, may be added at pleasure. *Time.*—Rather more than 1 hour. *Average cost*, 3*d*.

GRAVY, Cheap, for Hashes, &c.

Ingredients.—Bones and trimmings of the cooked joint intended for hashing, ¼ teaspoonful of salt, ¼ teaspoonful of whole pepper, ¼ teaspoonful of whole allspice, a small faggot of savoury herbs, ½ head of celery, 1 onion, 1 oz. of butter, thickening, sufficient boiling water to cover the bones. *Mode.*—Chop the bones in small pieces, and put them in a stewpan, with the trimmings, salt, pepper, spice, herbs, and celery. Cover with boiling water, and let the whole simmer gently for 1½ or 2 hours. Slice and fry the onion in the butter till it is of a pale brown, and mix it gradually with the gravy made from the bones; boil for ¼ hour, and strain into a basin; now put it back into the stewpan; flavour with walnut pickle or ketchup, pickled-onion liquor, or any store sauce that may be preferred. Thicken with a little butter and flour, kneaded together on a plate, and the gravy will be ready for use. After the thickening is added, the gravy should just boil, to take off the rawness of the flour. *Time.*—2 hours, or rather more. *Average cost*, 4*d.*, exclusive of the bones and trimmings.

GRAVY for Roast Meat.

Ingredients.—Gravy, salt. *Mode.*—Put a common dish with a small quantity of salt in it under the meat, about a quarter of an hour before it is removed from the fire. When the dish is full, take it away, baste the meat, and pour the gravy into the dish on which the joint is to be served.

GRAVY for Venison.

Ingredients.—Trimmings of venison, 3 or 4 mutton shank-bones, salt to taste, 1 pint of water, 2 teaspoonfuls of walnut ketchup. *Mode.*—Brown the trimmings over a nice clear fire, and put them in a stewpan with the shank-bones and water; simmer gently for 2 hours, strain and skim, and add the walnut ketchup and a seasoning of salt. Let it just boil, when it is ready to serve. *Time.*—2 hours.

GRAVY, Jugged (Excellent).

Ingredients.—2 lbs. of shin of beef, ¼ lb. of lean ham, 1 onion or a few shalots, 2 pints of water, salt and whole pepper to taste, 1 blade of mace, a faggot of savoury herbs, ½ a large carrot, ½ a head of celery. *Mode.*—Cut up the beef and ham into small pieces, and slice the vegetables; take a jar, capable of holding two pints of water, and arrange therein, in layers, the ham, meat, vegetables, and seasoning, alternately, filling up with the above quantity of water; tie down the jar, or put a plate over the top, so that the steam may not escape; place it in the oven, and let it remain there from 6 to

8 hours; should, however, the oven be very hot, less time will be required. When sufficiently cooked, strain the gravy, and when cold, remove the fat. It may be flavoured with ketchup, wines, or any other store sauce that may be preferred. It is a good plan to put the jar in a cool oven over-night, to draw the gravy; and then it will not require so long baking the following day. *Time.*—From 6 to 8 hours, according to the oven. *Average cost*, 7*d.* per pint.

GRAVY-KETTLE.

This is a utensil which will not be found in every kitchen; but it is a useful one where it is necessary to keep gravies hot for the purpose of pouring over various dishes as they are cooking. It is made of copper, and should, consequently, be heated over the hot-plate, if there be one, or a charcoal stove.

GRAVY-KETTLE.

GRAVY made without Meat for Fowls.

Ingredients.—The necks, feet, livers, and gizzards of the fowls, 1 slice of toasted bread, ½ onion, 1 faggot of savoury herbs, salt and pepper to taste, ½ pint of water, thickening of butter and flour, 1 dessertspoonful of ketchup. *Mode.*—Wash the feet of the fowls thoroughly clean, and cut them and the neck into small pieces. Put these into a stewpan with the bread, onion, herbs, seasoning, livers, and gizzards; pour the water over them and simmer gently for 1 hour. Now take out the liver, pound it, and strain the liquor to it. Add a thickening of butter and flour, and a flavouring of mushroom ketchup; boil it up and serve. *Time.*—1 hour. *Average cost*, 4*d.* per pint.

GRAVY, Rich, for Hashes, Ragoûts, &c.

Ingredients.—2 lbs. of shin of beef, 1 large onion or a few shalots, a little flour, a bunch of savoury herbs, 2 blades of mace, 2 or 3 cloves, 4 whole allspice, ¼ teaspoonful of whole pepper, 1 slice of lean ham or bacon, ½ a head of celery (when at hand), 2 pints of boiling water; salt and cayenne to taste. *Mode.*—Cut, the beef into thin slices, as also the onions, dredge them with flour, and fry of a pale brown, but do not allow them to get black; pour in the boiling water, let it boil up, and skim. Add the remaining ingredients, and simmer the whole very gently for 2 hours, or until all the juices are extracted from the meat; put it by to get cold, when take off all the fat. This gravy may be flavoured with ketchup, store sauces, wine, or, in fact, anything that may give additional and suitable relish to the dish it is intended for. *Time.*—Rather more than 2 hours. *Average cost*, 8*d*. per pint.

GRAVY SOUP.

Ingredients.—6 lbs. of shin of beef, a knuckle of veal weighing 5 lbs., a few pieces or trimmings, 2 slices of nicely-flavoured lean ham; ¼ lb. of butter, 4 onions, 4 carrots, 1 turnip, nearly a head of celery, 3 blades of mace, 6 cloves, a bunch of savoury herbs, seasoning of salt and pepper to taste, 3 lumps of sugar, 6 quarts of boiling soft water. It can be flavoured with ketchup, Leamington sauce, Harvey's sauce, and a little soy. *Mode.*—Slightly brown the meat and ham in the butter, but do not let them burn. When this is done, pour to it the water, and as the scum rises, take it off; when no more appears, add all the other ingredients, and let the soup simmer slowly by the fire for 6 hours without stirring it any more from the bottom; take it off, and let it settle; skim off all the fat you can, and pass it through a sieve or cloth. When perfectly cold you can remove all the fat, and leave the sediment untouched, which serves very nicely for thick gravies, hashes, &c. *Time.*—7 hours. *Average cost*, 1*s*. per quart. *Seasonable* all the year. *Sufficient* for 14 persons.

GRAVY, Veal, for White Sauces, Fricassees, &c.

Ingredients.—2 slices of nicely-flavoured lean ham, any poultry trimmings, 3 lbs. of lean veal, a faggot of savoury herbs, including parsley, a few green onions (or 1 large onion may be substituted for these), a few mushrooms, when obtainable; 1 blade of mace, salt to taste, 3 pints of water. *Mode.*—Cut up the ham and veal into small square pieces, put these in a stewpan, moistening them with a small quantity of water; place them over the fire to draw down. When the bottom of the stewpan becomes covered with a white glaze, fill up with water in the above proportion; add the remaining ingredients, stew very slowly for 3 or 4 hours, and do not forget to skim well the moment it boils. Put it by, and when cold take off all the fat. This may be used for Béchamel, sauce tournée, and many other white sauces. *Time.*—3 or 4 hours. *Average cost*, 9*d.* per pint.

GREENGAGE JAM.

Ingredients.—To every lb. of fruit, weighed before being stoned, allow ¾ lb. of lump sugar. *Mode.*—Divide the greengages, take out the stones, and put them into a preserving-pan. Bring the fruit to a boil, then add the sugar, and keep stirring it over a gentle fire until it is melted. Remove all the scum as it rises, and, just before the jam is done, boil it rapidly for 5 minutes. To ascertain when it is sufficiently boiled, pour a little on a plate, and if the syrup thickens and appears firm, it is done. Have ready half the kernels blanched; put them into the jam, give them one boil, and pour the preserve into pots. When cold, cover down with oiled papers, and, over these, tissue paper brushed over on both sides with the white of an egg. *Time.*—¾ hour after the sugar is added. *Average cost*, from 6*d.* to 8*d.* per lb. pot. *Sufficient.*—Allow about 1½ pint of fruit for every lb. pot of jam. *Seasonable.*—Make this in August or September.

GREENGAGES, Compôte of.

Ingredients.—1 pint of syrup, 1 quart of greengages. *Mode.*—Make a syrup, skim it well, and put in the greengages when the syrup is boiling, having previously removed the stalks and stones from the fruit. Boil gently for ¼ hour, or until the fruit is tender; but take care not to let it break, as the appearance of the dish would be spoiled were the fruit reduced to a pulp. Take the greengages carefully out, place them on a glass dish, boil the syrup for another 5 minutes, let it cool a little, pour over the fruit, and, when cold, it will be ready for use. *Time.*—¼ hour to simmer the fruit, 5 minutes the syrup. *Average cost*, in full season, 10*d.* *Sufficient* for 4 or 5 persons. *Seasonable* in July, August, and September.

GREENGAGES, to Preserve and Dry.

Ingredients.—To every lb. of sugar allow 1 lb. of fruit, ¼ pint of water. *Mode.*—For this purpose, the fruit must be used before it is quite ripe, and part of the stalk must be left on. Weigh the fruit, rejecting all that is in the least degree blemished, and put it into a lined saucepan with the sugar and water, which should have been previously boiled together to a rich syrup. Boil the fruit in this for 10 minutes, remove it from the fire, and drain the greengages. The next day, boil up the syrup and put in the fruit again, and let it simmer for 3 minutes, and drain the syrup away. Continue this process for 5 or 6 days, and the last time place the greengages, when drained, on a hair sieve, and put them in an oven or warm spot to dry; keep them in a box, with paper between each layer, in a place free from damp. *Time.*—10 minutes the first time of boiling. *Seasonable.*—Make this in August or September.

GREENGAGES, Preserved in Syrup.

Ingredients.—To every lb. of fruit allow 1 lb. of loaf sugar, ¼ pint of water. *Mode.*—Boil the sugar and water together for about 10 minutes; divide the greengages, take out the stones, put the fruit into the syrup, and let it simmer gently until nearly tender. Take it off the fire, put it into a large pan, and, the next day, boil it up again for about 10 minutes with the kernels from the stones, which should be blanched. Put the fruit carefully into jars, pour over it the syrup, and, when cold, cover down, so that the air is quite excluded. Let the syrup be well skimmed both the first and second day of boiling, otherwise it will not be clear. *Time.*—10 minutes to boil the syrup; ¼ hour to simmer the fruit the first day, 10 minutes the second day. *Average cost*, from 6*d.* to 8*d.* per lb. pot. *Sufficient.*—Allow about 1 pint of fruit to fill a 1-lb. pot. *Seasonable.*—Make this in August or September.

GREENS, Boiled Turnip.

Ingredients.—To each ½ gallon of water allow 1 heaped tablespoonful of salt; turnip-greens. *Mode.*—Wash the greens well in two or three waters, and pick off all the decayed and dead leaves; tie them in small bunches, and put them into plenty of boiling water, salted in the above proportion. Keep them boiling quickly, with the lid of the saucepan uncovered, and when tender, pour them into a colander; let them drain, arrange them in a vegetable-dish, remove the string that the greens were tied with, and serve. *Time.*—15 to 20 minutes. *Average cost*, 4*d*. for a dish for 3 persons. *Seasonable* in March, April, and May.

GROUSE PIE.

Ingredients.—Grouse; cayenne, salt, and pepper to taste; 1 lb. of rump-steak, ½ pint of well-seasoned broth, puff-paste. *Mode.*—Line the bottom of a pie-dish with the rump-steak cut into neat pieces, and, should the grouse be large, cut them into joints; but, if small, they may be laid in the pie whole; season highly with salt, cayenne, and black pepper; pour in the broth, and cover with a puff-paste; brush the crust over with the yolk of an egg, and bake from ¾ to 1 hour. If the grouse is cut into joints, the backbones and trimmings will make the gravy, by stewing them with an onion, a little sherry, a bunch of herbs, and a blade of mace: this should be poured in after the pie is baked. *Time.*—¾ to 1 hour. *Average cost*, exclusive of the grouse, which are seldom bought, 1*s*. 9*d*. *Seasonable* from the 12th of August to the beginning of December.

ROAST GROUSE.

GROUSE, Roast.

Ingredients.—Grouse, butter, a thick slice of toasted bread. *Mode.*—Let the birds hang as long as possible; pluck and draw them; wipe, but do not wash them, inside and out, and truss them without the head, the same as for a roast fowl. Many persons still continue to truss them with the head under the wing, but the former is now considered the most approved method. Put them down to a sharp clear fire; keep them well basted the whole of the time they are cooking, and serve them on a buttered toast, soaked in the dripping-pan, with a little melted butter poured over them, or with bread-sauce and gravy. *Time.*—½ hour; if liked very thoroughly done, 35 minutes.

Average cost, 2*s*. to 2*s*. 6*d*. the brace; but seldom bought. *Sufficient.*—2 for a dish. *Seasonable* from the 12th of August to the beginning of December.

GROUSE, to Carve.

Grouse may be carved in the way first described in carving partridge. The backbone of the grouse is highly esteemed by many, and this part of many game birds is considered the finest-flavoured.

ROAST GROUSE.

GROUSE SALAD (Soyer's Recipe improved.)

Ingredients.—8 eggs, butter, fresh salad, 2 or 3 grouse; for the sauce, 1 tablespoonful of minced shalot, 2 tablespoonfuls of pounded sugar, the yolks of 2 eggs, 1 teaspoonful of minced parsley, ¼ oz. of salt, 12 tablespoonfuls of oil, 4 tablespoonfuls of Chili vinegar, 1 gill of cream, 2 tablespoonfuls of chopped tarragon and chervil. *Mode.*—Boil the eggs hard, shell them, throw them into cold water, cut a thin slice off the bottom to facilitate the proper placing of them in the dish, cut each one into four lengthwise, and make a very thin flat border of butter, about one inch from the edge of the dish the salad is to be served on; fix the pieces of egg upright close to each other, the yolk outside, or the yolk and white alternately; lay in the centre a fresh salad of whatever is in season, and, having previously roasted the grouse rather underdone, cut it into eight or ten pieces, and prepare the sauce as follows:—Put the shalots into a basin, with the sugar, the yolk of an egg, the parsley, and salt, and mix in by degrees the oil and vinegar; when all the ingredients are well mixed, put the sauce on ice or in a cool place. When ready to serve, whip the cream rather thick, which lightly mix with it; then lay the inferior parts of the grouse on the salad, sauce over so as to cover each piece, then lay over the salad and the remainder of the grouse, pour the rest of the sauce over, and serve. The eggs may be ornamented with a little dot of radishes or beetroot on the point. Anchovy and gherkin, cut into small diamonds, may be placed between, or cut gherkins in slices, and a border of them laid round. Tarragon or chervil-leaves are also a pretty addition. The remains of cold black-game, pheasant, or partridge may be used in the above manner, and will make a very delicate dish. *Average cost*, 2*s.* 6*d. Seasonable* from the 12th of August to the beginning of December.

GRUEL, to make.

Ingredients.—1 tablespoonful of Robinson's patent groats, 2 tablespoonfuls of cold water, 1 pint of boiling water. *Mode.*—Mix the prepared groats smoothly with the cold water in a basin; pour over them the boiling water, stirring it all the time. Put it into a very clean saucepan; boil the gruel for 10 minutes, keeping it well stirred; sweeten to taste, and serve. It may be flavoured with a small piece of lemon-peel, by boiling it in the gruel, or a little grated nutmeg may be put in; but in these matters the taste of the patient should be consulted. Pour the gruel in a tumbler, and serve. When wine is allowed to the invalid, 2 tablespoonfuls of sherry or port make this preparation very nice. In cases of colds, the same quantity of spirits is sometimes added instead of wine. *Time.*—10 minutes. *Sufficient* to make a pint of gruel.

GUDGEONS.

Ingredients.—Egg and bread-crumbs sufficient for the quantity of fish; hot lard. *Mode.*—Do not scrape off the scales, but take out the gills and inside, and cleanse thoroughly; wipe them dry, flour and dip them into egg, and sprinkle over with bread-crumbs. Fry of a nice brown. *Time.*—3 or 4 minutes. *Average cost.*—Seldom bought. *Seasonable* from March to July. *Sufficient.*—3 for each person.

GUINEA-FOWL, Roast, Larded.

Ingredients.—A guinea-fowl, lardoons, flour, and salt. *Mode.*—When this bird is larded, it should be trussed the same as a pheasant; if plainly roasted, truss it like a turkey. After larding and trussing it, put it down to roast at a brisk fire; keep it well basted, and a short time before serving, dredge it with a little flour, and let it froth nicely. Serve with a little gravy in the dish, and a tureen of the same, and one of well-made bread-sauce. *Time.*—Guinea-fowl, larded, 1¼ hour; plainly roasted, about 1 hour. *Sufficient* for 6 persons. *Seasonable* in winter.

Note.—The breast, if larded, should be covered with a piece of paper, and removed about 10 minutes before serving.

GURNET, or GURNARD.

Ingredients.—1 gurnet, 6 oz. of salt to each gallon of water. *Mode.*—Cleanse the fish thoroughly, and cut off the fins; have ready some boiling water, with salt in the above proportion; put the fish in, and simmer very gently for ½ hour. Parsley and butter, or anchovy sauce, should be served with it. *Time.*—¼ hour. *Average cost.*—Seldom bought. *Seasonable* from October to March, but in perfection in October. *Sufficient.*—A middling-sized one for two persons.

Note.—This fish is frequently stuffed with forcemeat, and baked.

HADDOCK, Baked.

Ingredients.—A nice forcemeat, butter to taste, egg and bread-crumbs. *Mode.*—Scale and clean the fish, without cutting it open much; put in a nice delicate forcemeat, and sew up the slit. Brush it over with egg, sprinkle over bread-crumbs, and baste frequently with butter. Garnish with parsley and cut lemon, and serve with, a nice brown gravy, plain melted butter, or anchovy sauce. The egg and bread-crumbs can be omitted, and pieces of butter placed over the fish. *Time.*—Large haddock, ¾ hour; moderate size, ¼ hour. *Seasonable* from August to February. *Average cost*, from 9*d.* upwards.

Note.—Haddocks may be filleted, rubbed over with egg and bread-crumbs, and fried a nice brown; garnish with crisped parsley.

HADDOCK, Boiled.

Ingredients.—Sufficient water to cover the fish; ¼ lb. of salt to each gallon of water. *Mode.*—Scrape the fish, take out the inside, wash it thoroughly, and lay it in a kettle, with enough water to cover it, and salt in the above proportion. Simmer gently from 15 to 20 minutes, or rather more, should the fish be very large. For small haddocks, fasten the tails in their mouths, and put them into boiling water. 10 to 15 minutes will cook them. Serve with plain melted butter, or anchovy sauce. *Time.*—Large haddock, ½ hour; small, ¼ hour, or rather less. *Average cost*, from 9*d.* upwards. *Seasonable* from August to February.

HADDOCK, Dried.

Dried haddock should be gradually warmed through, either before or over a nice clear fire. Rub a little piece of butter over, just before sending it to table.

HADDOCK, Dried.

Ingredients.—1 large thick haddock, 2 bay-leaves, 1 small bunch of savoury herbs, not forgetting parsley, a little butter and pepper; boiling water. *Mode.*—Cut up the haddock into square pieces, make a basin hot by means of hot water, which pour out. Lay in the fish, with the bay-leaves and herbs; cover with boiling water; put a plate over to keep in the steam, and let it remain for 10 minutes. Take out the slices, put them in a hot dish, rub over with butter and pepper, and serve. *Time.*—10 minutes. *Seasonable* at any time, but best in winter.

HAM OMELET (a delicious Breakfast Dish).

Ingredients.—6 eggs, 4 oz. of butter, ½ saltspoonful of pepper, 2 tablespoonfuls of minced ham. *Mode.*—Mince the ham very finely, without any fat, and fry it for 2 minutes in a little butter; then make the batter for the omelet, stir in the ham, and proceed as in the case of a plain omelet. Do not add any salt to the batter, as the ham is usually sufficiently salt to impart a flavour to the omelet. Good lean bacon, or tongue, answers equally well for this dish; but they must also be slightly cooked previously to mixing them with the batter. Serve very hot and quickly, without gravy. *Time.*—From 4 to 6 minutes. *Average cost*, 1s. *Sufficient* for 4 persons. *Seasonable* at any time.

HAM, FRIED, AND EGGS (a Breakfast Dish).

Ingredients.—Ham; eggs. *Mode.*—Cut the ham into slices, and take care that they are of the same thickness in every part. Cut off the rind, and if the ham should be particularly hard and salt, it will be found an improvement to soak it for about 10 minutes in hot water, and then dry it in a cloth. Put it into a cold frying-pan, set it over the fire, and turn the slices 3 or 4 times whilst they are cooking. When done, place them on a dish, which should be kept hot in front of the fire during the time the eggs are being poached. Poach the eggs, slip them on to the slices of ham, and serve quickly. *Time.*

—7 or 8 minutes to broil the ham. *Average cost,* 8*d.* to 1*s.* per lb. by the whole ham. *Sufficient.*—Allow 2 eggs and a slice of ham to each person. *Seasonable* at any time.

Note.—Ham may also be toasted or broiled; but, with the latter method, to insure its being well cooked, the fire must be beautifully clear, or it will have a smoky flavour far from agreeable.

HAM, Potted, that will keep Good for some time.

Ingredients.—To 4 lbs. of lean ham allow 1 lb. of fat, 2 teaspoonfuls of pounded mace, ½ nutmeg grated, rather more than ½ teaspoonful of cayenne, clarified lard. *Mode.*—Mince the ham, fat and lean together in the above proportion, and pound it well in a mortar, seasoning it with cayenne pepper, pounded mace, and nutmeg; put the mixture into a deep baking-dish, and bake for ½ hour; then press it well into a stone jar, till up the jar with clarified lard, cover it closely, and paste over it a piece of thick paper. If well seasoned, it will keep a long time in winter, and will be found very convenient for sandwiches, &c. *Time.*—½ hour. *Seasonable* at any time.

HAM, Potted (a nice addition to the Breakfast or Luncheon table).

Ingredients.—To 2 lbs. of lean ham allow ½ lb. of fat, 1 teaspoonful of pounded mace, ½ teaspoonful of pounded allspice, ½ nutmeg, pepper to taste, clarified butter. *Mode.*—Cut some slices from the remains of a cold ham, mince them small, and to every 2 lbs. of lean allow the above proportion of fat. Pound the ham in a mortar to a fine paste, with the fat, gradually add the seasonings and spices, and be very particular that all the ingredients are well mixed and the spices well pounded. Press the mixture into potting-pots, pour over clarified butter, and keep it in a cool place. *Average cost* for this quantity, 2*s.* 6*d. Seasonable* at any time.

HAM, to Bake.

Ingredients.—Ham; a common crust. *Mode.*—As a ham for baking should be well soaked, let it remain in water for at least 12 hours. Wipe it dry, trim away any rusty places underneath, and cover it with a common crust, taking care that this is of sufficient thickness all over to keep the gravy in. Place it in a moderately-heated oven, and bake for nearly 4 hours. Take off the crust and skin, and cover with raspings, the same as for boiled ham, and garnish the knuckle with a paper frill. This method of cooking a ham is, by many persons, considered far superior to boiling it, as it cuts fuller of gravy and has a finer flavour, besides keeping a much longer time good. *Time.*—A medium-sized ham, 4 hours. *Average cost*, from 8*d.* to 1*s.* per lb. by the whole ham. *Seasonable* all the year.

HAM, to Boil.

BOILED HAM.

Ingredients.—Ham, water, glaze, or raspings. *Mode.*—In choosing a ham, ascertain that it is perfectly sweet, by running a sharp knife into it, close to the bone; and if, when the knife is withdrawn, it has an agreeable smell, the ham is good; if, on the contrary, the blade has a greasy appearance and offensive smell, the ham is bad. If it has been long hung, and is very dry and salt, let it remain in soak for 24 hours, changing the water frequently. This length of time is only necessary in the case of its being very hard; from 8 to 12 hours would be sufficient for a Yorkshire or Westmoreland ham. Wash it thoroughly clean, and trim away from the under-side all the rusty and smoked parts, which would spoil the appearance. Put it into a boiling-pot, with sufficient cold water to cover it; bring it gradually to boil, and as the scum rises, carefully remove it. Keep it simmering very gently until tender, and be careful that it does not stop boiling, nor boil too quickly. When done, take it out of the pot, strip off the skin, and sprinkle over it a few fine bread-raspings, put a frill of cut paper round the knuckle, and serve. If to be eaten cold, let the ham remain in the water until nearly cold: by this method the juices are kept in, and it will be found infinitely superior to one taken out of the water hot; it should, however, be borne in mind that the ham must *not* remain in the saucepan *all* night. When the skin is removed, sprinkle over bread-raspings, or, if wanted particularly nice, glaze it. Place a paper frill round the knuckle, and garnish with parsley or cut vegetable flowers. *Time.*—A ham weighing 10 lbs., 4 hours to *simmer gently*; 15 lbs., 5 hours; a very large one, about 6 hours. *Average cost*, from 8*d.* to 1*s.* per lb. by the whole ham. *Seasonable* all the year.

HAM, how to Boil to give it an excellent flavour.

Ingredients.—Vinegar and water, 2 heads of celery, 2 turnips, 3 onions, a large bunch of savoury herbs. *Mode.*—Prepare the ham as in the preceding recipe, and let it soak for a few hours in vinegar and water. Put it on in cold water, and when it boils, add the vegetables and herbs. Simmer very gently until tender, take it out, strip off the skin, cover with bread-raspings, and put a paper ruche or frill round the knuckle. *Time.*—A ham weighing 10 lbs., 4 hours. *Average cost*, 8*d.* to 1*s.* per lb. by the whole ham. *Seasonable* at any time.

HAM, to Carve.

In cutting a ham, the carver must be guided according as he desires to practise economy, or have, at once, fine slices out of the prime part. Under the first supposition, he will commence at the knuckle end, and cut off thin slices towards the thick part of the ham. To reach the choicer portion, the knife, which must be very sharp and thin, should be carried quite down to the bone, in the direction of the line 1 to 2. The slices should be thin and even, and always cut down to the bone. There are some who like to carve a ham by cutting a hole at the top, and then slicing pieces off inside the hole, gradually enlarging the circle; but we think this is a plan not to be recommended. A ham, when hot, is usually sent to table with a paper ruffle round the knuckle.

HAM.

HAMS, for Curing (Mons. Ude's Recipe).

Ingredients.—For 2 hams weighing about 16 or 18 lbs. each, allow 1 lb. of moist sugar, 1 lb. of common salt, 2 oz. of saltpetre, 1 quart of good vinegar. *Mode.*—As soon as the pig is cold enough to be cut up, take the 2 hams and rub them well with common salt, and leave them in a large pan for 3 days. When the salt has drawn out all the blood, drain the hams, and throw the brine away. Mix sugar, salt, and saltpetre together in the above proportion, rub the hams well with these, and put them into a vessel large enough to hold them, always keeping the salt over them. Let them remain for 3 days, then pour over them a quart of good vinegar. Turn them in the brine every day for a month, then drain them well, and rub them with bran. Have them smoked over a wood fire, and be particular that the hams are hung as high up as possible from the fire; otherwise the fat will melt, and they will become dry and hard. *Time.*—To be pickled 1 month; to be smoked 1 month. *Sufficient* for 2 hams of 18 lbs. each. *Seasonable* from October to March.

HAMS, to Cure Sweet, in the Westmoreland way.

Ingredients.—3 lbs. of common salt, 3 lbs. of coarse sugar, 1 lb. of bay-salt, 3 quarts of strong beer. *Mode.*—Before the hams are put into pickle, rub them the preceding day well with salt, and drain the brine well from them. Put the above ingredients into a saucepan, and boil for ¼ hour; pour over the hams, and let them remain a month in the pickle. Rub and turn them every day, but do not take them out of the pickling-pan; and have them smoked for a month. *Time.*—To be pickled 1 month; to be smoked 1 month. *Seasonable* from October to March.

HAMS, to Pickle (Suffolk Recipe).

Ingredients.—To a ham from 10 to 12 lbs., allow 1 lb. of coarse sugar, ¾ lb. of salt, 1 oz. of saltpetre, ½ a teacupful of vinegar. *Mode.*—Rub the hams well with common salt, and leave them for a day or two to drain; then rub well in the above proportion of sugar, salt, saltpetre, and vinegar, and turn them every other day. Keep them in the pickle 1 month, drain them, and send them to be smoked over a wood fire for 3 weeks or a month. *Time.*—To remain in the pickle 1 month; to be smoked 3 weeks or 1 month.

Sufficient.—The above proportion of pickle is sufficient for 1 ham. *Seasonable.*—Hams should be pickled from October to March.

HAMS, to Salt Two, about 12 or 15 lbs. each.

Ingredients.—2 lbs. of treacle, ½ lb. of saltpetre, 1 lb. of bay-salt, 2 pounds of common salt. *Mode.*—Two days before they are put into pickle, rub the hams well with salt, to draw away all slime and blood. Throw what comes from them away, and then rub them with treacle, saltpetre, and salt. Lay them in a deep pan, and let them remain one day; boil the above proportion of treacle, saltpetre, bay-salt, and common salt for ¼ hour, and pour this pickle boiling hot over the hams: there should be sufficient of it to cover them. For a day or two rub them well with it; afterwards they will only require turning. They ought to remain in this pickle for 3 weeks or a month, and then be sent to be smoked, which will take nearly or quite a month to do. An ox-tongue pickled in this way is most excellent, to be eaten either green or smoked. *Time.*—To remain in the pickle 3 weeks or a month; to be smoked about a month. *Seasonable* from October to March.

HAMS, to Smoke, at Home.

Take an old hogshead, stop up all the crevices, and fix a place to put a cross-stick near the bottom, to hang the articles to be smoked on. Next, in the side, cut a hole near the top, to introduce an iron pan filled with sawdust and small pieces of green wood. Having turned the tub upside down, hang the articles upon the cross-stick, introduce the iron pan in the opening, and place a piece of red-hot iron in the pan, cover it with sawdust, and all will be complete. Let a large ham remain 40 hours, and keep up a good smoke. Fish may be smoked in the same manner.

HARE, Broiled (a Supper or Luncheon Dish).

Ingredients.—The legs and shoulders of a roast hare, cayenne and salt to taste, a little butter. *Mode.*—Cut the legs and shoulders from a roast hare, season them highly with salt and cayenne, and broil them over a very clear fire for 5 minutes. Dish them on a hot dish, rub over them a little cold butter, and send to table very quickly. *Time.*—5 minutes. *Seasonable* from September to the end of February.

HARE, Hashed.

[Cold Meat Cookery.] *Ingredients.*—The remains of cold roast hare, 1 blade of pounded mace, 2 or 3 allspice, pepper and salt to taste, 1 onion, a bunch of savoury herbs, 3 tablespoonfuls of port wine, thickening of butter and flour, 2 tablespoonfuls of mushroom ketchup. *Mode.*—Cut the cold hare into neat slices, and put the head, bones, and trimmings into a stewpan, with ¾ pint of water; add the mace, allspice, seasoning, onion, and herbs, and stew for nearly an hour, and strain the gravy; thicken it with butter and flour, add the wine and ketchup, and lay in the pieces of hare, with any stuffing that may be left. Let the whole gradually heat by the side of the fire, and, when it has simmered for about 5 minutes, serve, and garnish the dish with sippets of toasted bread. Send red-currant jelly to table with it. *Time.*—Rather more than 1 hour. *Average cost*, exclusive of the cold hare, 6*d*. *Seasonable* from September to the end of February.

HARE, Jugged (very good).

Ingredients.—1 hare, 1½ lb. of gravy beef, ½ lb. of butter, 1 onion, 1 lemon, 6 cloves; pepper, cayenne, and salt to taste; ½ pint of port wine. *Mode.*—Skin, paunch, and wash the hare, cut it into pieces, dredge them with flour, and fry in boiling butter. Have ready 1½ pint of gravy, made from the above proportion of beef, and thickened with a little flour. Put this into a jar; add the pieces of fried hare, an onion stuck with six cloves, a lemon peeled and cut in half, and a good seasoning of pepper, cayenne, and salt; cover the jar down tightly, put it up to the neck into a stewpan of boiling water, and let it stew until the hare is quite tender, taking care to keep the water boiling. When nearly done, pour in the wine, and add a few forcemeat balls: these must be fried or baked in the oven for a few minutes before they are put to the gravy. Serve with red-currant jelly. *Time.*—3½ to 4 hours. If the hare is very old, allow 4½ hours. *Average cost*, 7*s*. *Sufficient* for 7 or 8 persons. *Seasonable* from September to the end of February.

HARE, Jugged (a Quicker and more Economical Way).

Ingredients.—1 hare, a bunch of sweet herbs, 2 onions, each stuck with 3 cloves, 6 whole allspice, ½ teaspoonful of black pepper, a strip of lemon-peel, thickening of butter and flour, 2 tablespoonfuls of mushroom ketchup,

¼ pint of port wine. *Mode.*—Wash the hare nicely, cut it up into joints (not too large), and flour and brown them as in the preceding recipe; then put them into a stewpan with the herbs, onions, cloves, allspice, pepper, and lemon-peel; cover with hot water, and when it boils, carefully remove all the scum, and let it simmer gently till tender, which will be in about 1¾ hour, or longer, should the hare be very old. Take out the pieces of hare, thicken the gravy with flour and butter, add the ketchup and port wine, let it boil for about 10 minutes, strain it through a sieve over the hare, and serve. A few fried forcemeat balls should be added at the moment of serving, or, instead of frying them, they may be stewed in the gravy, about 10 minutes before the hare is wanted for table. Do not omit to serve red-currant jelly with it. *Time.*—Altogether 2 hours. *Average cost,* 5*s.* 6*d. Sufficient* for 7 or 8 persons. *Seasonable* from September to the end of February.

Note.—Should there be any left, re-warm it the next day by putting the hare, &c., into a covered jar, and placing this jar in a saucepan of boiling water; this method prevents a great deal of waste.

HARE, Potted (a Luncheon or Breakfast Dish).

Ingredients.—1 hare, a few slices of bacon, a large bunch of savoury herbs, 4 cloves, ½ teaspoonful of whole allspice, 2 carrots, 2 onions, salt and pepper to taste, 1 pint of water, 2 glasses of sherry. *Mode.*—Skin, empty, and wash the hare; cut it down the middle, and put it into a stewpan, with a few slices of bacon under and over it; add the remaining ingredients, and stew very gently until the hare is tender, and the flesh will separate easily from the bones. When done enough, take it up, remove the bones, and pound the meat, *with the bacon,* in a mortar, until reduced to a perfectly smooth paste. Should it not be sufficiently seasoned, add a little cayenne, salt, and pounded mace, but be careful that these are well mixed with the other ingredients. Press the meat into potting-pots, pour over clarified butter, and keep in a dry place. The liquor that the hare was stewed in, should be saved for hashes, soups, &c. &c. *Time.*—About 2½ hours to stew the hare. *Seasonable* from September to the end of February.

HARE, Roast.

ROAST HARE.

Ingredients.—Hare, forcemeat, a little milk, butter. *Choosing and Trussing.*—Choose a young hare; which may be known by its smooth and sharp claws, and by the cleft in the lip not being much spread. To be eaten in perfection, it must hang for some time; and, if properly taken care of, it may be kept for several days. It is better to hang without being paunched; but should it be previously emptied, wipe the inside every day, and sprinkle over it a little pepper and ginger, to prevent the musty taste which long keeping in the damp occasions, and also which affects the stuffing. After it is skinned, wash it well, and soak for an hour in warm water to draw out the blood; if old, let it lie in vinegar for a short time, but wash it well afterwards in several waters. Make a forcemeat, wipe the hare dry, fill the belly with it, and sew it up. Bring the hind and fore legs close to the body towards the head, run a skewer through each, fix the head between the shoulders by means of another skewer, and be careful to leave the ears on. Put a string round the body from skewer to skewer, and tie it above the back. *Mode.*— The hare should be kept at a distance from the fire when it is first laid down, or the outside will become dry and hard before the inside is done. Baste it well with milk for a short time, and afterwards with butter; and particular attention must be paid to the basting, so as to preserve the meat on the back juicy and nutritive. When it is almost roasted enough, flour the hare, and baste well with butter. When nicely frothed, dish it, remove the skewers, and send it to table with a little gravy in the dish, and a tureen of the same. Red-currant jelly must also not be forgotten, as this is an indispensable accompaniment to roast hare. For economy, good beef dripping may be substituted for the milk and butter to baste with; but the basting, as we have before stated, must be continued without intermission. If the liver is good, it may be parboiled, minced, and mixed with the stuffing; but it should not be used unless quite fresh. *Time.*—A middling-sized hare, 1¼ hour; a large hare, 1½ to 2 hours. *Average cost,* from 4s. to 6s. *Sufficient* for 5 or 6 persons. *Seasonable* from September to the end of February.

HARE, Roast, to Carve.

The "Grand Carver" of olden times, a functionary of no ordinary dignity, was pleased when he had a hare to manipulate, for his skill and grace had an opportunity of display. *Diners à la Russe* may possibly, erewhile, save modern gentlemen the necessity of learning the art which was in auld lang syne one of the necessary accomplishments of the youthful squire; but, until side-tables become universal, or till we see the office of "grand carver" once more instituted, it will be well for all to learn how to assist at the carving of this dish, which, if not the most elegant in appearance, is a very general favourite. The hare, having its head to the left, as shown in the woodcut, should be first served by cutting slices from each side of the backbone, in the direction of the lines from 3 to 4. After these prime parts are disposed of, the leg should next be disengaged by cutting round the line indicated by the figures 5 to 6. The shoulders will then be taken off by passing the knife round from 7 to 8. The back of the hare should now be divided by cutting quite through its spine, as shown by the line 1 to 2, taking care to feel with the point of the knife for a joint where the back may be readily penetrated. It is the usual plan not to serve any bone in helping hare; and thus the flesh should be sliced from the legs and placed alone on the plate. In large establishments, and where men-cooks are kept, it is often the case that the backbone of the hare, especially in old animals, is taken out, and then the process of carving is, of course, considerably facilitated. A great point to be remembered in connection with carving hare is, that plenty of gravy should accompany each helping, otherwise this dish, which is naturally dry, will lose half its flavour, and so become a failure. Stuffing is also served with it; and the ears, which should be nicely crisp, and the brains of the hare, are esteemed as delicacies by many connoisseurs.

ROAST HARE.

HARE SOUP.

Ingredients.—A hare fresh-killed, 1 lb. of lean gravy-beef, a slice of ham, 1 carrot, 2 onions, a faggot of savoury herbs, ¼ oz. of whole black pepper, a little browned flour, ¼ pint of port wine, the crumb of two French rolls, salt and cayenne to taste, 3 quarts of water. *Mode.*—Skin and paunch the hare, saving the liver and as much blood as possible. Cut it in pieces, and put it in a stewpan with all the ingredients, and simmer gently for 6 hours. This soup should be made the day before it is wanted. Strain through a sieve, put the best parts of the hare in the soup, and serve.

HARE SOUP.

Proceed as above; but, instead of putting the joints of the hare in the soup, pick the meat from the bones, pound it in a mortar, and add it, with the crumb of two French rolls, to the soup. Rub all through a sieve; heat slowly, but do not let it boil. Send it to table immediately. *Time.*—8 hours. *Average cost*, 1*s.* 9*d.* per quart. *Seasonable* from September to February. *Sufficient* for 10 persons.

HERB POWDER, for Flavouring when Fresh Herbs are not obtainable.

Ingredients.—1 oz. of dried lemon-thyme, 1 oz. of dried winter savory, 1 oz. of dried sweet marjoram and basil, 2 oz. of dried parsley, 1 oz. of dried lemon-peel. *Mode.*—Prepare and dry the herbs, pick the leaves from the stalks, pound them, and sift them through a hair sieve; mix in the above proportions, and keep in glass bottles, carefully excluding the air. This we think a far better method of keeping herbs, as the flavour and fragrance do not evaporate so much as when they are merely put in paper bags. Preparing them in this way, you have them ready for use at a moment's notice. Mint, sage, parsley, &c., dried, pounded, and each put into separate bottles, will be found very useful in winter.

HERBS, to Dry, for Winter Use.

On a very dry day, gather the herbs, just before they begin to flower. If this is done when the weather is damp, the herbs will not be so good a colour. (It is very necessary to be particular in little matters like this, for trifles constitute perfection, and herbs nicely dried will be found very acceptable when frost and snow are on the ground. It is hardly necessary, however, to state that the flavour and fragrance of fresh herbs are incomparably finer.) They should be perfectly freed from dirt and dust, and be divided into small bunches, with their roots cut off. Dry them quickly in a very hot oven, or before the fire, as by this means most of their flavour will be preserved, and be careful not to burn them; tie them up in paper bags, and keep in a dry place. This is a very general way of preserving dried herbs; but we would recommend the plan described in a former recipe. *Seasonable.*—From the month of July to the end of September is the proper time for storing herbs for winter use.

HERRINGS, White, Baked.

Ingredients.—12 herrings, 4 bay-leaves, 12 cloves, 12 allspice, 2 small blades of mace, cayenne pepper and salt to taste, sufficient vinegar to fill up the dish. *Mode.*—Take herrings, cut off the heads, and gut them. Put them in a pie-dish, heads and tails alternately, and, between each layer, sprinkle over the above ingredients. Cover the fish with the vinegar, and bake for ½ hour, but do not use it till quite cold. The herrings may be cut down the front, the backbone taken out, and closed again. Sprats done in this way are very delicious. *Time.*—½ an hour. *Average cost*, 1*d.* each.

To Choose the Herring.—The more scales this fish has, the surer the sign of its freshness. It should also have a bright and silvery look; but if red about the head, it is a sign that it has been dead for some time.

HERRINGS, Red or YARMOUTH BLOATERS.

The best way to cook these is to make incisions in the skin across the fish, because they do not then require to be so long on the fire, and will be far better than when cut open. The hard roe makes a nice relish by pounding it in a mortar, with a little anchovy, and spreading it on toast. If very dry, soak in warm water 1 hour before dressing.

HIDDEN MOUNTAIN, The (a pretty Supper Dish).

Ingredients.—6 eggs, a few slices of citron, sugar to taste, ¼ pint of cream, a layer of any kind of jam. *Mode.*—Beat the whites and yolks of the eggs separately; then mix them and beat well again, adding a few thin slices of citron, the cream, and sufficient pounded sugar to sweeten it nicely. When the mixture is well beaten, put it into a buttered pan, and fry the same as a pancake; but it should be three times the thickness of an ordinary pancake. Cover it with jam, and garnish with slices of citron and holly-leaves. This dish is served cold. *Time.*—About 10 minutes to fry the mixture. *Average cost*, with the jam, 1*s.* 4*d*. *Sufficient* for 3 or 4 persons. *Seasonable* at any time.

HODGE-PODGE.

Ingredients.—2 lbs. of shin of beef, 3 quarts of water, 1 pint of table-beer, 2 onions, 2 carrots, 2 turnips, 1 head of celery; pepper and salt to taste; thickening of butter and flour. *Mode.*—Put the meat, beer, and water in a stewpan; simmer for a few minutes, and skim carefully. Add the vegetables and seasoning; stew gently till the meat is tender. Thicken with the butter and flour, and serve with turnips and carrots, or spinach and celery. *Time.*—3 hours, or rather more. *Average cost*, 3*d*. per quart. *Seasonable* at any time. *Sufficient* for 12 persons.

HODGE-PODGE.

[COLD MEAT COOKERY.] *Ingredients.*—About 1 lb. of underdone cold mutton, 2 lettuces, 1 pint of green peas, 5 or 6 green onions, 2 oz. of butter, pepper and salt to taste, ½ teacupful of water. *Mode.*—Mince the mutton, and cut up the lettuces and onions in slices. Put those in a stewpan, with all the ingredients except the peas, and let these simmer very gently for ¾ hour, keeping them well stirred. Boil the peas separately, mix these with the mutton, and serve very hot. *Time.*—¾ hour. *Sufficient* for 3 or 4 persons. *Seasonable* from the end of May to August.

HOLLY-LEAVES, to Frost, for Garnishing and Decorating Dessert and Supper Dishes.

Ingredients.—Sprigs of holly, oiled butter, coarsely-powdered sugar. *Mode.*—Procure some nice sprigs of holly; pick the leaves from the stalks, and wipe them with a clean cloth free from all moisture; then place them on a dish near the fire, to get thoroughly dry, but not too near to shrivel the leaves; dip them into oiled butter, sprinkle over them some coarsely-powdered sugar, and dry them before the fire. They should be kept in a dry place, as the least damp would spoil their appearance. *Time.*—About 10 minutes to dry before the fire. *Seasonable.*—These may be made at any time; but are more suitable for winter garnishes, when fresh flowers are not easily obtained.

HONEY CAKE.

Ingredients.—½ breakfast-cupful of sugar, 1 breakfast-cupful of rich sour cream, 2 breakfast-cupfuls of flour, ½ teaspoonful of carbonate of soda, honey to taste. *Mode.*—Mix the sugar and cream together; dredge in the flour, with as much honey as will flavour the mixture nicely; stir it well that all the ingredients may be thoroughly mixed; add the carbonate of soda, and beat the cake well for another 5 minutes; put it into a buttered tin, bake it from ½ to ¾ hour, and let it be eaten warm. *Time.*—½ to ¾ hour. *Average cost*, 8d. *Sufficient* for 3 or 4 persons. *Seasonable* at any time.

HORSERADISH.

This root, scraped, is always served with hot roast beef, and is used for garnishing many kinds of boiled fish. Let the horseradish remain in cold water for an hour; wash it well, and with a sharp knife scrape it into very thin shreds, commencing from the thick end of the root. Arrange some of it lightly in a small glass dish, and the remainder use for garnishing the joint; it should be placed in tufts round the border of the dish, with 1 or 2 bunches on the meat. *Average cost*, 2d. per stick. *Seasonable* from October to June.

HORSERADISH SAUCE, to serve with Roast Beef.

Ingredients.—4 tablespoonfuls of grated horseradish, 1 teaspoonful of pounded sugar, 1 teaspoonful of salt, ½ teaspoonful of pepper, 2 teaspoonfuls of made mustard; vinegar. *Mode.*—Grate the horseradish, and mix it well with the sugar, salt, pepper, and mustard; moisten it with sufficient vinegar to give it the consistency of cream, and serve in a tureen; 3 or 4 tablespoonfuls of cream added to the above very much improve the appearance and flavour of this sauce. To heat it to serve with hot roast beef, put it in a *bain marie* or a jar, which place in a saucepan of boiling water; make it hot, but do not allow it to boil, or it will curdle.

Note.—This sauce is a great improvement on the old-fashioned way of serving cold-scraped horseradish with hot roast beef. The mixing of the cold vinegar with the warm gravy cools and spoils everything on the plate. Of course, with cold meat, the sauce should be served cold.

HORSERADISH VINEGAR.

Ingredients.—¼ lb. of scraped horseradish, 1 oz. of minced shalot, 1 drachm of cayenne, 1 quart of vinegar. *Mode.*—Put all the ingredients into a bottle, which shake well every day for a fortnight. When it is thoroughly steeped, strain and bottle, and it will be fit for use immediately. This will be found an agreeable relish to cold beef, &c. *Seasonable.*—This vinegar should be made either in October or November, as horseradish is then in its highest perfection.

HOT SPICE (a Delicious Adjunct to Chops, Steaks, Gravies, &c.)

Ingredients.—3 drachms each of ginger, black pepper, and cinnamon, 7 cloves, ½ oz. mace, ¼ oz. of cayenne, 1 oz. grated nutmeg, 1½ oz. white pepper. *Mode.*—Pound the ingredients, and mix them thoroughly together, taking care that everything is well blended. Put the spice in a very dry glass bottle for use. The quantity of cayenne may be increased, should the above not be enough to suit the palate.

ICE-CREAMS, Fruit.

Ingredients.—To every pint of fruit-juice allow 1 pint of cream; sugar to taste. *Mode.*—Let the fruit be well ripened; pick it off the stalks, and put it into a large earthen pan. Stir it about with a wooden spoon, breaking it until it is well mashed; then, with the back of the spoon, rub it through a hair sieve. Sweeten it nicely with pounded sugar; whip the cream for a few minutes, add it to the fruit, and whisk the whole again for another 5 minutes. Put the mixture into the freezing-pot, and freeze, taking care to stir the cream, &c., two or three times, and to remove it from the sides of the vessel, that the mixture may be equally frozen and smooth. Ices are usually served in glasses, but if moulded, as they sometimes are for dessert, must have a small quantity of melted isinglass added to them, to enable them to keep their shape. Raspberry, strawberry, currant, and all fruit ice-creams, are made in the same manner. A little pounded sugar sprinkled over the fruit before it is mashed assists to extract the juice. In winter, when fresh fruit is not obtainable, a little jam may be substituted for it: it should be melted and worked through a sieve before being added to the whipped cream; and if the colour should not be good, a little prepared, cochineal or beetroot may be put in to improve its appearance. *Time.*—½ hour to freeze the mixture. *Average cost*, with cream at 1*s*. per pint, 4*d*. each ice. *Seasonable*, with fresh fruit, in June, July, and August.

ICE, Lemon-water.

Ingredients.—To every pint of syrup, allow 1/3 pint of lemon-juice; the rind of 4 lemons. *Mode.*—Rub the sugar on the rinds of the lemons, and with it make the syrup. Strain the lemon-juice, add it to the other ingredients, stir well, and put the mixture into a freezing-pot. Freeze as directed for Ice Pudding, and when the mixture is thoroughly and equally frozen, put it into ice-glasses. *Time.*—½ hour to freeze the mixture. *Average cost*, 3*d*. to 4*d*. each. *Seasonable* at any time.

ICED-PUDDING (Parisian Recipe).

ICED-PUDDING MOULD.

Ingredients.—½ lb. of sweet almonds, 2 oz. of bitter ones, ¾ lb, of sugar, 8 eggs, 1½ pint of milk. *Mode.*—Blanch and dry the almonds thoroughly in a cloth, then pound them in a mortar until reduced to a smooth paste; add to these the well-beaten eggs, the sugar, and milk; stir these ingredients over the fire until they thicken, but do not allow them to boil; then strain and put the mixture into the freezing-pot; surround it with ice, and freeze it. When quite frozen, fill an iced-pudding mould, put on the lid, and keep the pudding in ice until required for table; then turn it out on the dish, and garnish it with a *compôte* or any fruit that may be preferred, pouring a little over the top of the pudding. This pudding may be flavoured with vanilla, Curaçoa, or Maraschino. *Time.*—½ hour to freeze the mixture. *Seasonable.* —Served all the year round.

ICES.

Ices are composed, it is scarcely necessary to say, of congealed cream or water, combined sometimes with liqueurs or other flavouring ingredients, or more generally with the juices of fruits. At desserts, or at some evening parties, ices are scarcely to be dispensed with. The principal utensils required for making ice-creams are ice-tubs, freezing-pots, spaddles, and a cellaret. The tub must be large enough to contain about a bushel of ice, pounded small, when brought out of the ice-house, and mixed very carefully with either *salt, nitre,* or *soda.* The freezing-pot is best made of pewter. If it be of tin, as is sometimes the case, the congelation goes on too rapidly in it for the thorough intermingling of its contents, on which the excellence of the ice greatly depends. The spaddle is generally made of copper, kept bright and clean. The cellaret is a tin vessel, in which ices are kept for a short time from dissolving. The method to be pursued in the freezing process must be attended to. When the ice-tub is prepared with fresh-pounded ice and salt, the freezing-pot is put into it up to its cover. The articles to be congealed are then poured into it and covered over; but to prevent the ingredients from separating and the heaviest of them from falling to the bottom of the mould, it is requisite to turn the freezing-pot round and round by the handle, so as to keep its contents moving until the congelation commences. As soon as this is perceived (the cover of the pot being occasionally taken off for the purpose of noticing when freezing takes place), the cover is immediately closed over it, ice is put upon it, and it is left in this state till it is served. The use of the spaddle is to stir up and remove from the sides of the freezing-pot the cream, which in the shaking may have washed against it, and by stirring it in with the rest, to prevent waste of it occurring. Any negligence in stirring the contents of the freezing-pot before congelation takes place, will destroy the whole: either the sugar sinks to the bottom and leaves the ice insufficiently sweetened, or lumps are formed, which disfigure and discolour it.

ICES, to make Fruit-water.

Ingredients.—To every pint of fruit-juice allow 1 pint of syrup. *Mode.*— Select nice ripe fruit; pick off the stalks and put it into a large earthen pan, with a little pounded sugar strewed over; stir it about with a wooden spoon until it is well broken, then rub it through a hair sieve. Make a syrup, without white of egg; let it cool add the fruit-juice, mix well together, and put the mixture into the freezing-pot. Proceed as directed for Ice Puddings, and when the mixture is equally frozen, put it into small glasses. Raspberry, strawberry, currant, and other fresh-fruit-water ices, are made in the same manner. *Time.*—½ hour to freeze the mixture. *Average cost,* 3*d.* to 4*d.* each. *Seasonable,* with fresh fruit, in June, July, and August.

DISH OF ICES.

ICING, Almond, for Cakes.

Ingredients.—To every lb. of finely-pounded loaf sugar, allow 1 lb. of sweet almonds, the whites of 4 eggs, a little rosewater. *Mode.*—Blanch the almonds, and pound them (a few at a time) in a mortar to a paste, adding a little rosewater to facilitate the operation. Whisk the whites of the eggs to a strong froth; mix them with the pounded almonds, stir in the sugar, and beat altogether. When the cake is sufficiently baked, lay on the almond icing, and put it into the oven to dry. Before laying this preparation on the cake, great care must be taken that it is nice and smooth, which is easily accomplished by well beating the mixture.

ICING, Sugar, for Cakes.

Ingredients.—To every lb. of loaf sugar allow the whites of 4 eggs, 1 oz. of fine starch. *Mode.*—Beat the eggs to a strong froth, and gradually sift in the sugar, which should be reduced to the finest possible powder, and gradually add the starch, also finely powdered. Beat the mixture well until the sugar is smooth; then with a spoon or broad knife lay the ice equally over the cakes. These should then be placed in a very cool oven, and the icing allowed to dry and harden, but not to colour. The icing may be coloured with strawberry or currant juice, or with prepared cochineal. If it be put on the cakes as soon as they are withdrawn from the oven, it will become firm and hard by the time the cakes are cold. On very rich cakes, such as wedding, christening cakes, &c., a layer of almond icing is usually spread over the top, and over that the white icing as described. All iced cakes should be kept in a very dry place.

INVALID COOKERY.

A few Rules to be observed in Cooking for Invalids.

Let all the kitchen utensils used in the preparation of invalids' cookery be delicately and *scrupulously clean*; if this is not the case, a disagreeable flavour may be imparted to the preparation, which flavour may disgust, and prevent the patient from partaking of the refreshment when brought to him or her.

For invalids, never make a large quantity *of one thing*, as they seldom require much at a time; and it is desirable that variety be provided for them.

Always have something in readiness; a little beef tea, nicely made and nicely skimmed, a few spoonfuls of jelly, &c., &c., that it may be administered as soon almost as the invalid wishes for it. If obliged to wait a long time, the patient loses the desire to eat, and often turns against the food when brought to him or her.

In sending dishes or preparations up to invalids, let everything look as tempting as possible. Have a clean tray-cloth laid smoothly over the tray; let the spoons, tumblers, cups and saucers, &c., be very clean and bright. Gruel served in a tumbler is more appetizing than when served in a basin or cup and saucer.

As milk is an important article of food for the sick, in warm weather let it be kept on ice, to prevent its turning sour. Many other delicacies may also be preserved good in the same manner for some little time.

If the patient be allowed to eat vegetables, never send them up undercooked, or half raw; and let a small quantity only be temptingly arranged on a dish. This rule will apply to every preparation, as an invalid is much more likely to enjoy his food if small delicate pieces are served to him.

Never leave food about a sick-room; if the patient cannot eat it when brought to him, take it away, and bring it to him in an hour or two's time. Miss Nightingale says, "To leave the patient's untasted food by his side from meal to meal, in hopes that he will eat it in the interval, is simply to prevent him from taking any food at all." She says, "I have known patients literally incapacitated from taking one article of food after another by this piece of ignorance. Let the food come at the right time, and be taken away, eaten or uneaten, at the right time, but never let a patient have 'something always standing' by him, if you don't wish to disgust him of everything."

Never serve beef tea or broth with the *smallest particle* of fat or grease on the surface. It is better, after making either of these, to allow them to get perfectly cold, when *all the fat* may be easily removed; then warm up as much as may be required. Two or three pieces of clean whity-brown paper laid on the broth will absorb any greasy particles that may be floating at the top, as the grease will cling to the paper.

Roast mutton, chickens, rabbits, calves' feet or head, game, fish (simply dressed), and simple puddings, are all light food, and easily digested. Of course, these things are only partaken of supposing the patient is recovering.

A mutton chop, nicely cut, trimmed, and broiled to a turn, is a dish to be recommended for invalids; but it must not be served *with all the fat* at the end, nor must it be too thickly cut. Let it be cooked over a fire free from smoke, and sent up with the gravy in it, between two very hot plates. Nothing is more disagreeable to an invalid than *smoked* food.

In making toast-and-water, never blacken the bread, but toast it only a nice brown. Never leave toast-and-water to make until the moment it is required, as it cannot then be properly prepared,—at least the patient will be obliged to drink it warm, which is anything but agreeable.

In boiling eggs for invalids, let the white be just set; if boiled hard, they will be likely to disagree with the patient.

In Miss Nightingale's admirable "Notes on Nursing," a book that no mother or nurse should be without, she says,—"You cannot be too careful as to quality in sick-diet. A nurse should never put before a patient milk that is sour, meat or soup that is turned, an egg that is bad, or vegetables underdone." Yet often, she says, she has seen these things brought in to the sick, in a state perfectly perceptible to every nose or eye except the nurse's. It is here that the clever nurse appears,—she will not bring in the peccant article; but, not to disappoint the patient, she will whip up something else in a few minutes. Remember, that sick-cookery should half do the work of your poor patient's weak digestion.

She goes on to caution nurses, by saying,—"Take care not to spill into your patient's saucer; in other words, take care that the outside bottom rim of his cup shall be quite dry and clean. If, every time he lifts his cup to his lips, he has to carry the saucer with it, or else to drop the liquid upon and to soil his sheet, or bedgown, or pillow, or, if he is sitting up, his dress, you have no idea what a difference this minute want of care on your part makes to his comfort, and even to his willingness for food."

INVALID'S CUTLET.

Ingredients.—1 nice cutlet from a loin or neck of mutton; 2 teacupfuls of water; 1 very small stick of celery; pepper and salt to taste. *Mode.*—Have the cutlet cut from a very nice loin or neck of mutton, take off all the fat, put it into a stewpan with the other ingredients; stew very gently indeed for nearly 2 hours, and skim off every particle of fat that may rise to the surface from time to time. The celery should be out into thin slices before it is added to the meat, and care must be taken not to put in too much of this, or the dish will not be good. If the water is allowed to boil fast, the cutlet will be hard. *Time.*—2 hours very gentle stewing. *Average cost*, 6*d*. *Sufficient* for one person. *Seasonable.*—Whenever celery may be had.

INVALID'S JELLY.

Ingredients.—12 shanks of mutton, 3 quarts of water, a bunch of sweet herbs, pepper and salt to taste, 3 blades of mace, 1 onion, 1 lb. of lean beef, a crust of bread toasted brown. *Mode.*—Soak the shanks in plenty of water for some hours, and scrub them well; put them, with the beef and other ingredients, into a saucepan with the water, and let them simmer very gently for 5 hours. Strain the broth, and, when cold, take off all the fat. It may be eaten either warmed up or cold as a jelly. *Time.*—5 hours. *Average cost*, 1*s*. *Sufficient* to make from 1½ to 2 pints of jelly. *Seasonable* at any time.

INVALIDS, Lemonade for.

Ingredients.—½ lemon, lump sugar to taste, 1 pint of boiling water. *Mode.*—Pare off the rind of the lemon thinly; cut the lemon into 2 or 3 thick slices, and remove as much as possible of the white outside pith, and all the pips. Put the slices of lemon, the peel, and lump sugar into a jug; pour over the boiling water; cover it closely, and in 2 hours it will be fit to drink. It should either be strained or poured off from the sediment. *Time.*—2 hours. *Average cost*, 2*d*. *Sufficient* to make 1 pint of lemonade. *Seasonable* at any time.

JAM ROLY-POLY PUDDING.

Ingredients.—¾ lb. of suet-crust, ¾ lb. of any kind of jam. *Mode.*—Make a nice light suet-crust, and roll it out to the thickness of about ½ inch. Spread the jam equally over it, leaving a small margin of paste without any, where the pudding joins. Roll it up, fasten the ends securely, and tie it in a floured cloth; put the pudding into boiling water, and boil for 2 hours. Mincemeat or marmalade may be substituted for the jam, and makes excellent puddings. *Time.*—2 hours. *Average cost*, 9*d*. *Sufficient* for 5 or 6 persons. *Seasonable.*—Suitable for winter puddings, when fresh fruit is not obtainable.

JANUARY—BILLS OF FARE.

Dinner for 18 persons.

First Course.

Entrées.

Dinner for 12 persons.

First Course.—Carrot soup à la Crécy; ox-tail soup; turbot and lobster sauce; fried smelts, with Dutch sauce. *Entrées.* Mutton cutlets, with Soubise sauce; sweetbreads; oyster patties; fillets of rabbits. *Second Course.*—Roast Turkey; stewed rump of beef à la jardinière; boiled ham, garnished with Brussels sprouts; boiled chickens and celery sauce. *Third course.*—Roast hare; teal; eggs à la neige; vol-au-vent of preserved fruit; 1 jelly; 1 cream; potatoes à la maître d'hôtel; grilled mushrooms; dessert and ices.

Dinner for 10 persons.

First Course.—Soup à la Reine; whitings au gratin; crimped cod and oyster sauce. *Entrées.*—Tendrons de veau; curried fowl and boiled rice. *Second Course.*—Turkey, stuffed with chestnuts, and chestnut sauce; boiled leg of mutton, English fashion, with caper sauce and mashed turnips. *Third course.*—Woodcocks or partridges; widgeon; Charlotte à la vanille; cabinet pudding; orange jelly; blancmange; artichoke bottoms; macaroni, with Parmesan cheese; dessert and ices.

Dinner for 8 persons.

First course.—Mulligatawny soup; brill and shrimp sauce; fried whitings. *Entrées.*—Fricasseed chicken; pork cutlets, with tomato sauce. *Second course.*—Haunch of mutton; boiled turkey and celery sauce; boiled tongue, garnished with Brussels sprouts. *Third Course.*—Roast pheasants; meringues à la crême; compôte of apples; orange jelly, cheesecakes; soufflé of rice; dessert and ices.

Dinners for 6 persons.

First Course.—Julienne soup; soles à la Normandie. *Entrées.*—Sweetbreads, with sauce piquante; mutton cutlets, with mashed potatoes. *Second Course.*—Haunch of venison; boiled fowls and bacon, garnished with Brussels sprouts. *Third Course.*—Plum pudding; custards in glasses; apple tart; fondue à la Brillat Savarin; dessert.

First Course.—Vermicelli soup; fried slices of codfish and anchovy sauce; John Dory. *Entrées.*—Stewed rump-steak à la jardinière; rissoles; oyster patties. *Second Course.*—Leg of mutton; curried rabbit and boiled rice. *Third Course.*—Partridges; apple fritters; tartlets of greengage jam; orange jelly; plum-pudding; dessert.

First Course.—Pea-soup; baked haddock; soles à la crême. *Entrées.*—Mutton cutlets and tomato sauce; fricasseed rabbit. *Second Course.*—Roast pork and apple sauce; breast of veal, rolled and stuffed; vegetables. *Third Course.*—Jugged hare; whipped cream; blancmange; mince pies; cabinet pudding.

First Course.—Palestine soup; fried smelts; stewed eels. *Entrées.*—Ragoût of lobster; broiled mushrooms; vol-au-vent of chicken. *Second Course.*—Sirloin of beef; boiled fowls and celery sauce; tongue, garnished with Brussels sprouts. *Third Course.*—Wild ducks; Charlotte aux pommes; cheesecakes; transparent jelly, inlaid with brandy cherries; blancmange; Nesselrode pudding.

JANUARY, Plain Family Dinners for.

Sunday.—1. Boiled turbot and oyster sauce, potatoes. 2. Roast leg or griskin of pork, apple sauce, brocoli, potatoes. 3. Cabinet pudding, and damson tart made with preserved damsons.

Monday.—1. The remains of turbot warmed in oyster sauce, potatoes. 2. Cold pork, stewed steak. 3. Open jam tart, which should have been made with the pieces of paste left from the damson tart; baked arrowroot pudding.

Tuesday.—1. Boiled neck of mutton, carrots, mashed turnips, suet dumplings, and caper sauce: the broth should be served first, and a little rice or pearl barley should be boiled in it along with the meat. 2. Rolled jam pudding.

Wednesday.—1. Roast rolled ribs of beef, greens, potatoes, and horseradish sauce. 2. Bread-and-butter pudding, cheesecakes.

Thursday.—1. Vegetable soup (the bones from the ribs of beef should be boiled down with this soup), cold beef, mashed potatoes. 2. Pheasants, gravy, bread sauce. 3. Macaroni.

Friday.—1. Fried whitings or soles. 2. Boiled rabbit and onion sauce, minced beef, potatoes. 3. Currant dumplings.

Saturday.—1. Rump-steak pudding or pie, greens, and potatoes. 2. Baked custard pudding and stewed apples.

Sunday.—1. Codfish and oyster sauce, potatoes. 2. Joint of roast mutton, either leg, haunch, or saddle; brocoli and potatoes, red-currant jelly. 3. Apple tart and custards, cheese.

Monday.—1. The remains of codfish picked from the bone, and warmed through in the oyster sauce; if there is no sauce left, order a few oysters and make a little fresh; and do not let the fish boil, or it will be watery. 2. Curried rabbit, with boiled rice served separately, cold mutton, mashed potatoes. 3. Somersetshire dumplings with wine sauce.

Tuesday.—1. Boiled fowls, parsley-and-butter; bacon garnished with Brussels sprouts; minced or hashed mutton. 2. Baroness pudding.

Wednesday.—1. The remains of the fowls cut up into joints and fricasseed; joint of roast pork and apple sauce, and, if liked, sage-and-onion, served on a dish by itself; turnips and potatoes. 2. Lemon pudding, either baked or boiled.

Thursday.—1. Cold pork and jugged hare, red-currant jelly, mashed potatoes. 2. Apple pudding.

Friday.—1. Boiled beef, either the aitchbone or the silver side of the round; carrots, turnips, suet dumplings, and potatoes: if there is a marrow-bone, serve the marrow on toast at the same time. 2. Rice snowballs.

Saturday.—1. Pea-soup made from liquor in which beef was boiled; cold beef, mashed potatoes. 2. Baked batter fruit pudding.

JANUARY, Things in Season.

Fish.—Barbel, brill, carp, cod, crabs, crayfish, dace, eels, flounders, haddocks, herrings, lampreys, lobsters, mussels, oysters, perch, pike, plaice, prawns, shrimps, skate, smelts, soles, sprats, sturgeon, tench, thornback, turbot, whitings.

Meat.—Beef, house lamb, mutton, pork, veal, venison.

Poultry.—Capons, fowls, tame pigeons, pullets, rabbits, turkeys.

Game.—Grouse, hares, partridges, pheasants, snipe, wild-fowl, woodcock.

Vegetables.—Beetroot, brocoli, cabbages, carrots, celery, chervil, cresses, cucumbers (forced), endive, lettuces, parsnips, potatoes, savoys, spinach, turnips, various herbs.

Fruit.—Apples, grapes, medlars, nuts, oranges, pears, walnuts, crystallized preserves (foreign), dried fruits, such as almonds and raisins; French and Spanish plums; prunes, figs, dates.

JAUNEMANGE.

Ingredients.—1 oz. of isinglass, 1 pint of water, ½ pint of white wine, the rind and juice of 1 large lemon, sugar to taste, the yolks of 6 eggs. *Mode.*—Put the isinglass, water, and lemon-rind into a saucepan, and boil gently until the former is dissolved; then add the strained lemon-juice, the wine, and sufficient white sugar to sweeten the whole nicely. Boil for 2 or 3 minutes, strain the mixture into a jug, and add the yolks of the eggs, which should be well beaten; place the jug in a saucepan of boiling water; keep stirring the mixture *one way* until it thickens, *but do not allow it to boil*; then take it off the fire, and keep stirring until nearly cold. Pour it into a mould, omitting the sediment at the bottom of the jug, and let it remain until quite firm. *Time.*—¼ hour to boil the isinglass and water; about 10 minutes to stir the mixture in the jug. *Average cost*, with the best isinglass, 2*s.* 9*d.* *Sufficient* to fill a quart mould. *Seasonable* at any time.

JELLIES

Are not the nourishing food they were at one time considered to be, and many eminent physicians are of opinion that they are less digestible than the flesh, or muscular part of animals; still, when acidulated with lemon-juice and flavoured with wine, they are very suitable for some convalescents. Vegetable jelly is a distinct principle, existing in fruits, which possesses the property of gelatinizing when boiled and cooled; but it is a principle entirely different from the gelatine of animal bodies, although the name of jelly, common to both, sometimes leads to an erroneous idea on that subject. Animal jelly, or gelatine, is glue, whereas vegetable jelly is rather analogous to gum. Liebig places gelatine very low indeed in the scale of usefulness. He says, "Gelatine, which by itself is tasteless, and when eaten, excites nausea, possesses no nutritive value; that, even when accompanied by the savoury constituents of flesh, it is not capable of supporting the vital process, and when added to the usual diet as a substitute for plastic matter, does not increase, but on the contrary, diminishes the nutritive value of the food, which it renders insufficient in quantity and inferior in quality." It is this substance which is most frequently employed in the manufacture of the jellies supplied by the confectioner; but those prepared at home from calves' feet do possess some nutrition, and are the only sort that should be given to invalids. Isinglass is the purest variety of gelatine, and is prepared from the sounds or swimming-bladders of certain fish, chiefly the sturgeon. From its whiteness it is mostly used for making blancmange and similar dishes.

JELLIES, Bottled, How to Mould.

Uncork the bottle; place it in a saucepan of hot water until the jelly is reduced to a liquid state; taste it, to ascertain whether it is sufficiently flavoured, and if not, add a little wine. Pour the jelly into moulds which have been soaked in water; let it set, and turn it out by placing the mould in hot water for a minute; then wipe the outside, put a dish on the top, and turn it over quickly. The jelly should then slip easily away from the mould, and be quite firm. It may be garnished as taste dictates.

JELLY, Isinglass, or Gelatine.

(Substitutes for Calf's Feet.)

Ingredients.—3 oz. of isinglass or gelatine, 2 quarts of water. *Mode.*—Put the isinglass or gelatine into a saucepan with the above proportion of cold water; bring it quickly to boil, and let it boil very fast, until the liquor is reduced one-half. Carefully remove the scum as it rises, then strain it through a jelly-bag, and it will be ready for use. If not required very clear, it may be merely strained through a fine sieve, instead of being run through a bag. Rather more than ½ oz. of isinglass is about the proper quantity to use for a quart of strong calf's-feet stock, and rather more than 2 oz. for the same quantity of fruit juice. As isinglass varies so much in quality and strength, it is difficult to give the exact proportions. The larger the mould, the stiffer should be the jelly; and where there is no ice, more isinglass must be used than if the mixture were frozen. This forms a stock for all kinds of jellies, which may be flavoured in many ways. *Time.*—1½ hour. *Sufficient*, with wine, syrup, fruit, &c., to fill two moderate-sized moulds. *Seasonable* at any time.

Note.—The above, when boiled, should be perfectly clear, and may be mixed warm with wine, flavourings, fruits, &c., and then run through the bag.

JELLY-BAG, How to make a.

JELLY-BAG.

The very stout flannel called double-mill, used for ironing-blankets, is the best material for a jelly-bag: those of home manufacture are the only ones to be relied on for thoroughly clearing the jelly. Care should be taken that the seam of the bag be stitched twice, to secure it against unequal filtration. The most convenient mode of using the bag is to tie it upon a hoop the exact size of the outside of its mouth; and, to do this, strings should be sewn round it at equal distances. The jelly-bag may, of course, be made any size; but one of twelve or fourteen inches deep, and seven or eight across the mouth, will be sufficient for ordinary use. The form of a jelly-bag is the fool's-cap.

JELLY Moulded with fresh Fruit, or Macedoine de Fruits.

Ingredients.—Rather more than 1½ pint of jelly, a few nice strawberries, or red or white currants, or raspberries, or any fresh fruit that may be in season. *Mode.*—Have ready the above proportion of jelly, which must be very clear and rather sweet, the raw fruit requiring an additional quantity of sugar. Select ripe, nice-looking fruit; pick off the stalks, unless currants are used, when they are laid in the jelly as they come from the tree. Begin by putting a little jelly at the bottom of the mould, which must harden; then arrange the fruit round the sides of the mould, recollecting that *it will be reversed when turned out*; then pour in some more jelly to make the fruit adhere, and, when that layer is set, put another row of fruit and jelly until the mould is full. If convenient, put it in ice until required for table, then wring a cloth in boiling water, wrap it round the mould for a minute, and turn the jelly carefully out. Peaches, apricots, plums, apples, &c., are better for being boiled in a little clear syrup before they are laid in the jelly; strawberries, raspberries, grapes, cherries, and currants are put in raw. In winter, when fresh fruits are not obtainable, a very pretty jelly may be made with preserved fruits or brandy cherries: these, in a bright and clear jelly, have a very pretty effect; of course, unless the jelly be *very clear*, the beauty of the dish will be spoiled. It may be garnished with the same fruit as is laid in the jelly; for instance, an open jelly with strawberries might have, piled in the centre, a few of the same fruit prettily arranged, or a little whipped cream might be substituted for the fruit. *Time.*—One layer of jelly should remain 2 hours in a very cool place, before another layer is added. *Average cost*, 2s. 6d. *Sufficient*, with fruit, to fill a quart mould. *Seasonable*, with fresh fruit, from June to October; with dried, at any time.

JELLY MOULDED WITH CHERRIES.

JELLY, ORANGE, Moulded with slices of Orange.

Ingredients.—1½ pint of orange jelly, 4 oranges, ½ pint of clarified syrup, *Mode.*—Boil ½ lb. of loaf sugar with ½ pint of water until there is no scum left (which must be carefully removed as fast as it rises), and carefully peel the oranges; divide them into thin slices, without breaking the thin skin, and put these pieces of orange into the syrup, where let them remain for about 5 minutes; then take them out, and use the syrup for the jelly. When the oranges are well drained, and the jelly is nearly cold, pour a little of the latter into the bottom of the mould; then lay in a few pieces of orange; over these pour a little jelly, and when this is set, place another layer of oranges, proceeding in this manner until the mould is full. Put it in ice, or in a cool place, and, before turning it out, wrap a cloth round the mould for a minute or two, which has been wrung out in boiling water. *Time.*—5 minutes to simmer the oranges, *Average cost,* 3*s.* 6*d. Sufficient,* with the slices of orange, to fill a quart mould. *Seasonable* from November to May.

JELLY of Two Colours.

JELLY OF TWO COLOURS.

Ingredients.—1½ pint of calf's-feet jelly, a few drops of prepared cochineal. *Mode.*—Make 1½ pint of calf's-feet jelly, or, if wished more economical, of clarified syrup and gelatine, flavouring it in any way that may be preferred. Colour one-half of the jelly with a few drops of prepared cochineal, and the other half leave as pale as possible. Have ready a mould well wetted in every part; pour in a small quantity of the red jelly, and let this set; when quite firm, pour on it the same quantity of the pale jelly, and let this set; then proceed in this manner until the mould is full, always taking care to let one jelly set before the other is poured in, or the colours would run one into the other. When turned out, the jelly should have a striped appearance. For variety, half the mould may be filled at once with one of the jellies, and, when firm, filled up with the other: this, also, has a very pretty effect, and is more expeditiously prepared than when the jelly is poured in small quantities into the mould. Blancmange and red jelly, or blancmange and raspberry cream, moulded in the above manner, look very well. The layers of blancmange and jelly should be about an inch in depth, and each layer should be perfectly hardened before another is added. Half a mould of blancmange and half a mould of jelly are frequently served in the same manner. A few pretty dishes may be made, in this way, of jellies or blancmanges left from the preceding day, by melting them separately in a jug placed in a saucepan of boiling water, and then moulding them by the foregoing directions. *Time.*—¾ hour to make the jelly. *Average cost*, with calf's-feet jelly, 2*s.*; with gelatine and syrup, more economical. *Sufficient* to fill 1½-pint mould. *Seasonable* at any time.

Note.—In making the jelly, use for flavouring a very pale sherry, or the colour will be too dark to contrast nicely with the red jelly.

JELLY, Open, with whipped Cream (a very pretty dish).

Ingredients.—1½ pint of jelly, ½ pint of cream, 1 glass of sherry, sugar to taste. *Mode.*—Make the above proportion of calf's-feet or isinglass jelly, colouring and flavouring it in any way that may be preferred; soak a mould, open in the centre, for about ½ hour in cold water; fill it with the jelly, and let it remain in a cool place until perfectly set; then turn it out on a dish; fill the centre with whipped cream, flavoured with sherry and sweetened with pounded sugar; pile this cream high in the centre, and serve. The jelly should be made of rather a dark colour, to contrast nicely with the cream. *Time.*—¾ hour. *Average cost*, 3*s.* 6*d. Sufficient* to fill 1½-pint mould. *Seasonable* at any time.

OPEN JELLY WITH WHIPPED CREAM.

JELLY, Savoury, for Meat Pies.

Ingredients.—3 lbs. of shin of beef, 1 calf's-foot, 3 lbs. of knuckle of veal, poultry trimmings (if for game pies, any game trimmings), 2 onions stuck with cloves, 2 carrots, 4 shalots, a bunch of savoury herbs, 2 bay-leaves; when liked, 2 blades of mace and a little spice; 2 slices of lean ham; rather more than 2 quarts of water. *Mode.*—Cut up the meat and put it into a stewpan with all the ingredients except the water; set it over a slow fire to draw down, and, when the gravy ceases to flow from the meat, pour in the water. Let it boil up, then carefully take away all scum from the top. Cover the stewpan closely, and let the stock simmer very gently for 4 hours: if rapidly boiled, the jelly will not be clear. When done, strain it through a fine sieve or flannel bag; and when cold, the jelly should be quite transparent. If this is not the case, clarify it with the whites of eggs. *Time.*—4 hours. *Average cost*, for this quantity, 5s.

JELLY, to make the Stock for, and to Clarify it.

Ingredients.—2 calf's feet, 6 pints of water. *Mode.*—The stock for jellies should always be made the day before it is required for use, as the liquor has time to cool, and the fat can be so much more easily and effectually removed when thoroughly set. Procure 2 nice calf's feet; scald them, to take off the hair; slit them in two, remove the fat from between the claws, and wash the feet well in warm water; put them into a stewpan, with the above proportion of cold water, bring it gradually to boil and remove every particle of scum as it rises. When it is well skimmed, boil it very gently for 6 or 7 hours, or until the liquor is reduced rather more than half; then strain it through a sieve into a basin, and put it in a cool place to set. As the liquor is strained, measure it, to ascertain the proportion for the jelly, allowing something for the sediment and fat at the top. To clarify it, carefully remove all the fat from the top, pour over a little warm water, to wash away any that may remain, and wipe the jelly with a clean cloth; remove the jelly from the sediment, put it into a saucepan, and, supposing the quantity to be a quart, add to it 6 oz. of loaf sugar, the shells and well-whisked whites of 5 eggs, and stir these ingredients together cold; set the saucepan on the fire, but *do not stir the jelly after it begins to warm.* Let it boil about 10 minutes after it rises to a head, then throw in a teacupful of cold water; let it boil 5 minutes longer, then take the saucepan off, cover it closely, and let it remain ½ hour near the fire. Dip the jelly-bag into hot water, wring it out quite dry, and fasten it on to a stand or the back of a chair, which must be placed near the fire, to prevent the jelly from setting before it has run through the bag. Place a basin underneath to receive the jelly; then pour it into the bag, and should it not be clear the first time, run it through the bag again. This stock is the foundation of all *really good* jellies, which may be varied in innumerable ways, by colouring and flavouring with liqueurs, and by moulding it with fresh and preserved fruits. To insure the jelly being firm when turned out, ½ oz. of isinglass clarified might be added to the above proportion of stock. Substitutes for calf's feet are now frequently used in making jellies, which lessen the expense and trouble in preparing this favourite dish, isinglass and gelatine being two of the principal materials employed; but although they may *look* as nicely as jellies made from good stock, they are never so delicate, having very often an unpleasant flavour, somewhat resembling glue, particularly when made with gelatine. *Time.*—About 6 hours to boil the feet for the stock; to clarify it,—¼ hour to boil, ½ hour to stand in the saucepan covered. *Average cost.*—Calf's feet may be purchased for 6*d.* each when veal is in full season, but more expensive when it is scarce. *Sufficient.*—2 calf's feet should make 1 quart of stock. *Seasonable* from March to October, but may be had all the year.

JELLY-MOULD.

JOHN DORY.

Ingredients.—-¼ lb. of salt to each gallon of water. *Mode.*—This fish, which is esteemed by most people a great delicacy, is dressed in the same way as a turbot, which it resembles in firmness, but not in richness. Cleanse it thoroughly and cut off the fins; lay it in a fish-kettle, cover with cold water, and add salt in the above proportion. Bring it gradually to a boil, and simmer gently for ¼ hour, or rather longer, should the fish be very large. Serve on a hot napkin, and garnish with cut lemon and parsley. Lobster, anchovy, or shrimp sauce, and plain melted butter, should be sent to table with it. *Time.*—After the water boils, ¼ to ½ hour, according to size. *Average cost*, 3*s.* to 5*s. Seasonable* all the year, but best from September to January.

Note.—Small John Dory are very good baked.

JUNE—BILLS OF FARE.

Dinner for 18 persons.

First Course.

Dessert and Ices.

Dinner for 12 persons.

First Course.—Green-pea soup; rice soup; salmon and lobster sauce; trout à la Genévése; whitebait. *Entrées.*—Lamb cutlets and cucumbers; fricasseed chicken; stewed veal and peas; lobster rissoles. *Second Course.*—Roast quarter of lamb and spinach; filet de bœuf à la Jardinière; boiled fowls; braised shoulder of lamb; tongue; vegetables. *Third Course.*—Goslings; ducklings; Nesselrode pudding; Charlotte à la Parisienne; gooseberry tartlets; strawberry cream; raspberry-and-currant tart; custards; dessert and ices.

Dinner for 10 persons.

First Course.—Julienne soup; salmon trout and parsley-and-butter; red mullet. *Entrées.*—Stewed breast of veal and peas; mutton cutlets à la Maintenon. *Second Course.*—Roast fillet of veal; boiled leg of lamb, garnished with young carrots; boiled bacon-cheek; vegetables. *Third Course.*—Roast ducks; leveret; gooseberry tart; strawberry cream; strawberry tartlets; meringues; cabinet pudding; iced pudding; dessert and ices.

Dinner for 8 persons.

First Course.—Vermicelli soup; trout à la Genévése; salmon cutlets. *Entrées.*—Lamb cutlets and peas; fricasseed chicken. *Second Course.*—Roast ribs of beef; half calf's head, tongue, and brains; boiled ham; vegetables. *Third Course.*—Roast ducks; compôte of gooseberries; strawberry jelly; pastry; iced pudding; cauliflower with cream sauce; dessert and ices.

Dinner for 6 persons.

First Course.—Spring soup; boiled salmon and lobster sauce. *Entrées.*—Veal cutlets and endive; ragoût of duck and green peas. *Second Course.*—Roast loin of veal; boiled leg of lamb and white sauce; tongue, garnished; vegetables. *Third Course.*—Strawberry cream; gooseberry tartlets; almond pudding; lobster salad; dessert.

First Course.—Calf's head soup; mackerel à la maître d'hôtel; whitebait. *Entrées.*—Chicken cutlets; curried lobster. *Second Course.*—Fore-quarter of lamb and salad; stewed beef à la Jardinière; vegetables. *Third Course.*—Goslings; green-currant tart; custards, in glasses; strawberry blancmange; soufflé of rice; dessert.

First Course.—Green-pea soup; baked soles aux fines herbes; stewed trout. *Entrées.*—Calf's liver and bacon; rissoles. *Second Course.*—Roast saddle of lamb and salad; calf's head à la tortue; vegetables. *Third Course.*—Roast ducks; vol-au-vent of strawberries and cream; strawberry tartlets; lemon blancmange; baked gooseberry pudding; dessert.

First Course.—Spinach soup; soles à la crême; red mullet. *Entrées.*—Roast fillet of veal; braised ham and spinach. *Second Course.*—Boiled fowls and white sauce; vegetables. *Third Course.*—Leveret; strawberry jelly; Swiss cream; cheesecakes; iced pudding; dessert.

JUNE, Plain Family Dinners for.

Sunday.—1. Salmon trout and parsley-and-butter, new potatoes. 2. Roast fillet of veal, boiled bacon-cheek and spinach, vegetables. 3. Gooseberry tart, custard.

Monday.—1. Light gravy soup. 2. Small meat pie, minced veal, garnished with rolled bacon, spinach, and potatoes. 3. Raspberry-and-currant tart.

Tuesday.—1. Baked mackerel, potatoes. 2. Boiled leg of lamb, garnished with young carrots. 3. Lemon pudding.

Wednesday.—1. Vegetable soup. 2. Calf's liver and bacon, peas, hashed lamb from remains of cold joint. 3. Baked gooseberry pudding.

Thursday.—1. Roast ribs of beef, Yorkshire pudding, peas, potatoes. 2. Stewed rhubarb and boiled rice.

Friday.—1. Cold beef and salad, lamb cutlets and peas. 2. Boiled gooseberry pudding and baked custard pudding.

Saturday.—1. Rump-steak pudding, broiled beef-bones and cucumber, vegetables. 2. Bread pudding.

Sunday.—1. Roast fore-quarter of lamb, mint sauce, peas, and new potatoes. 2. Gooseberry pudding, strawberry tartlets. Fondue.

Monday.—1. Cold lamb and salad, stewed neck of veal and peas, young carrots, and new potatoes. 2. Almond pudding.

Tuesday.—1. Green-pea soup. 2. Roast ducks stuffed, gravy, peas, and new potatoes. 3. Baked ratafia pudding.

Wednesday.—1. Roast leg of mutton, summer cabbage, potatoes. 2. Gooseberry and rice pudding.

Thursday.—1. Fried soles, melted butter, potatoes. 2. Sweetbreads, hashed mutton, vegetables. 3. Bread-and-butter pudding.

Friday.—1. Asparagus soup. 2. Boiled beef, young carrots, and new potatoes, suet dumplings. 3. College puddings.

end

www.ingramcontent.com/pod-product-compliance
Lightning Source LLC
Chambersburg PA
CBHW081626100526
44590CB00021B/3618